T0195591

EXPLORING A CHRISTIAN WORLDVIEW

How Does a Christian See the World?

Dr. Charles W. King

WESTBOW
PRESS®
A DIVISION OF THOMAS NELSON
& ZONDERVAN

Scripture taken from the American Standard Version of the Bible.

WestBow Press books may be ordered through booksellers or by contacting:

WestBow Press
A Division of Thomas Nelson & Zondervan
1663 Liberty Drive
Bloomington, IN 47403
www.westbowpress.com
1 (866) 928-1240

Because of the dynamic nature of the Internet, any web addresses or links contained in this book may have changed since publication and may no longer be valid. The views expressed in this work are solely those of the author and do not necessarily reflect the views of the publisher, and the publisher hereby disclaims any responsibility for them.

Any people depicted in stock imagery provided by Getty Images are models, and such images are being used for illustrative purposes only. Certain stock imagery © Getty Images.

ISBN: 978-1-9736-2382-3 (sc)
ISBN: 978-1-9736-2383-0 (hc)
ISBN: 978-1-9736-2381-6 (e)

Library of Congress Control Number: 2018903631

Print information available on the last page.

WestBow Press rev. date: 04/12/2018

Dr. King is a veteran of more than fifty years teaching in Christian colleges. He holds the Ph.D. degree from The University of Minnesota, candidacy for the Ph.D. degree from The University of Pittsburgh, is a graduate of Johnson Bible College and has done graduate study at School of Religion, Butler University.

His current email address is kingca@ roadrunner.com. Your comments would be appreciated.

He is the author of more than sixty articles in religious and professional periodicals and of books including:

Acts, Blueprint for the Church

Teaching Greek, the Comenius Method

Fifty Years in the Christian Ministry

The Mystery of the Tower and the Falls

ACKNOWLEDGEMENTS

A number of very good friends have contributed to the preparation of this book. They include Ruth Shannon Oder, a former editor for Standard Publishing, who did an editorial review of the book, the members of my Sunday school class at the Choatville Christian Church who have served as an editorial committee for the work, members of the Anderson Christian church who asked that I teach a short course in Christian World View in 2011 and my graduate school class in Christian World View at Blueridge College of Evangelism in the fall of 2011 who helped shape the course material into the background for this volume. .

None of my work would be possible without the patience, help and encouragement of my wife of fifty-nine years, Anna Lou (Rockey) King. She is a very important part of my "support system."

A NOTE TO GREEK READERS

In my early drafts, I used a number of Greek words using a "symbols" font. Later I recognized that the audience for this work is not primarily the Greek reading public, but a general one. Therefore, I have transliterated all of the Greek words into forms using the following rules. Transliterations appear in italics.

All of the consonants are transliterated by the corresponding English consonants. The zeta will have the "dz" usage within the word. A rough breathing will be represented by an "h". A double gamma is transliterated as "ng". The vowels are a bit more difficult. The following chart will indicate the transliterations.

Alpha — a	Epsilon — e	Eta — ee	Iota — i
Omicron— o	Upsilon — u	Omega — o̲ (Machen, 1928)	

The diphthongs are transliterated using the English letters as given for the vowels. This system is the same as that used for *The Word Study Concordance* (revision of *The New Englishman's Greek Concordance*) by George V. Wigram and Ralph D. Winter (1978) with one exception. Their transliterations distinguished the Omicron from the Omega by a line over the o which represented the Omega. My word processor does not have that element, so I have used an underlined "o" to represent the Omega.

ABBREVIATIONS USED

LXX refers to the Septuagint, a translation of the Hebrew Old Testament into Greek made by seventy Jewish scholars sometime in the three centuries before Christ. The Hellenistic Jews of Jesus days considered it an inspired translation. Some people today regard the King James Version in a similar way. I have no background in the Hebrew language. For this reason, all the quotations from Hebrew sources are from this Greek translation. It represents the best Jewish scholarship of Jesus' day.

SYSTEM OF DOCUMENTATION
USED IN THIS BOOK

A commonly accepted resource, *The Chicago Manual of Style*, (page 595, section 16.5) recognizes other systems of style, including those of the Modern Language Association, the American Psychological Association, and the American Medical Association. It states that some of the journals and serials it publishes use these or other styles

As a professor whose major teaching field is Psychology, and whose Ph.D. dissertation at the University of Minnesota used the American Psychological Association system it seems appropriate that I use the system used in my dissertation in this publication. The style will be that approved by the American Psychological Association in 1968.

The following are examples of complete citations included in that dissertation. These have reference to an attached Bibliography. The material within the parentheses is the complete footnote. All of these occur within the text, not at the bottom of the page.

(Cartter, 1966), Wilson (1942), (Young, 1949, p. 29), College Characteristic Index (CCI). Stecklein (1963, 1964), public law 918 (84th Congress, August 1956), Caplow and McGee study (1958), A. W. Dent (in Lee, 1967), Whitlock (n.d.)

This system enables the reader to find references if needed, but maintains the flow of the discussion with a minimum of distractions.

QUOTATIONS FROM THE BIBLE

All of the quotations from the Bible are taken from *The Holy Bible, Newly Edited by the American Revision Committee, A. D.1901.* New York: Thomas Nelson & Sons, 1901, commonly referred as the American Standard Version. (ASV)

I have elected to use this version because as a Greek professor I believe it best represents the grammar of the original Greek manuscripts. For most of a century many Greek teachers have reached a similar conclusion.

Occasionally, I have inserted my own translations where no English text seems to adequately represent the Greek originals. Most of these are third person imperatives, translation of the perfect tenses or occasions where I believe the middle voice (the subject acts on itself or with special regard to itself) is indicated. Other occasions are those where I prefer an alternate translation of a word.

CONTENTS

INTRODUCTORY REMARKS

When one considers the scope of the subject of a Christian World View, it at first seems overwhelming. The number of elements in a Christian world view seems enormous. Those persons who assisted in developing this work found a limited number of things which appear to be basic to the world view of an individual, though that person may not be aware of them. I believe we have located those central issues which constitute the framework of a Christian understanding of his world, the universe, the will of God and the inner "man" of a healthy Christian.

The fact that sincere Christians often differ on some of the issues has complicated the task. Because of this we decided that the study must begin with a statement of the concerns that should be foremost in the mind of the student who studies the Scriptures for guidance concerning these issues. The following is a set of guidelines for the study of the Scriptures and the opinions voiced in this volume. I vigorously urge the reader to remember them and use them consistently to test the content of the book and his understandings as he reads this volume.

RULES OF THE ROAD FOR THE CHRISTIAN STUDENT

I attempt to give you all the Scriptures actually say and avoid saying anything they do not say so that you can make an educated Christian judgment where that is possible. I am committed to the best use of the principles of good interpretation of any literature. We call this Hermeneutics when it concerns the Bible. I hope you will consistently apply these rules as you proceed. *Don't be discouraged by the complexity of what follows.* Grayson Ensign wrote a book on Hermeneutics entitled *"You Can Understand the Bible."* (1990) I believe he is correct and recommend his book.

Rules of Good Interpretation (Hermeneutics)

Every statement must be considered in the light of its context. (This rule is frequently violated when men go to the Scriptures seeking "proof texts" for what they want the Scriptures to teach.)

The context includes at least the following elements.

I.   Who is writing *or* speaking?
II. Who is the writer (or the speaker) addressing?
III. What is the purpose of the writer (or the speaker)? What was the writer (or the speaker) seeking to accomplish?
IV. What elements in the culture in which it is written are important to a correct understanding of what is written?

V. What elements in the immediate history, the broader unit of history, and in the whole scope of history affect the meaning?

VI. What place does the statement have within the Scriptures? This includes the context of:

1. the sentence,
2. the paragraph,
3. the division of the book,
4. the total book,
5. the total Bible,
6. the writings of the one who wrote it including the following:
   a) his personal history
   b) the problem he is facing when he wrote the passage
   c) his use of any element of language in any special way.

VII. What elements in the language are important to understanding the passage?

- What are the possible English *meanings* of the words used? (The complexity of this is easily seen when one uses a lexicon.)
- What are the biases of the translator? (This will determine the words he selects to translate from the original languages.)
- How does the structure of the sentences affect the meaning? In some senses the Grammar determines the meaning.
- What differences between Greek or Hebrew and English affect the meaning? In Greek the tenses are rather specific, and are not the same as in English. Greek has two tenses for which there are no English parallels. In contrast to English, the Greek has a third person imperative and a middle voice.
- What other passages deal with the issue? How can all the passages be understood in harmony with all others?

Obviously you will probably not personally have the resources for all of this background, but you should be able to find someone who will help you with critical passages. Some commentaries will help you, but be cautious of the bias of both the commentary and your helper. This includes the translators of the Bible you read.

All of these are simply the tools needed for the excellence in Biblical interpretation, which should be the object of any student of Scripture.

Additional Considerations in Handling Scripture

I am committed to five principles which are as follows.

- First, I will speak where the Scriptures speak.
- Second, I will be silent where the Scriptures are silent.
- Third, I will regard conclusions drawn from Scripture as possibly truly scriptural teaching, but as binding only on those who see them as being necessarily true. (This is a paraphrase of Thomas Campbell in "The Declaration and Address.") (Richardson, Vol. 1, page 259)
- Fourth, I will not allow differences concerning the third principle to create divisions in the church or between Christian brethren.
- Fifth, I will try to be aware of my own biases and their origin.

A Christian will seek to base his attitudes on scriptural teachings, not human opinions but will realize the truth of this statement, "That although inferences and deductions from Scripture premises, when fairly inferred, may be truly called the doctrine of God's Holy Word, yet are they not formally binding upon the conscience of Christians further than they perceive the connection, and evidently see that they are so, for their faith must not stand in the wisdom of men, but in the power and veracity of God." (Richardson, Vol. 1, p. 259) This will apply to a number of the items in this book.

A Christian in dealing with those who disagree will be careful to remember Jesus' statement in Matthew 7:1, 2, "for by what judgment you judge, ye shall be judged, and with what measure ye mete, it shall be measured unto you." He will be particularly concerned to avoid the curse which Jesus places on those who judge.

A Christian will in no way compromise the second greatest commandment. "Thou shalt love thy neighbor" should be especially applicable to relations between Christians. (1 John 4:7, 5:1) Permitting differences of opinion to cause divisions among Christians constitutes one of the greatest curses on the church. (1 Corinthians 3:1—4)

THE WORLD THROUGH CHRISTIAN EYES
INTRODUCTION

These discussions will attempt to describe the world as seen through the eyes of a Christian who knows and is committed to Biblical truth as the standard for faith and Christian living.

This is not a creed, but more a statement of Philosophy, stated in an informal and popular way. It is not however a complete philosophy. It is not a *Philosophy of the Christian Religion*. That would require much deeper and more profound study and statements. It is, preeminently an effort to indicate how a Christian sees the world when he takes into account all of the scriptural teaching he has at hand and attempts to use this information in evaluating the various options.

The central source of ideas and of authority for the views expressed is the Bible, particularly the New Testament. We make extensive reference to Biblical teaching in every area considered and attempt to be as complete as possible in the collection of data from Scripture for the analysis.

The author hopes that this may serve as an inspiration and guide to Christians in general and possibly as text materials for courses studying the Christian World View. *The author also wants to make it so direct and simple that the most ordinary person can comprehend and use it without needing to fear misunderstanding or making mistakes.*

CHAPTER 1

WHAT IS TRUTH? – WHAT CAN I DEPEND ON?

*W*e begin this discussion with an issue that is basic to the entire study; "What is truth?" This was Pilate's unanswered question (John 18:38) though in some senses the answer stood before him. It is, however, a fundamental question of Philosophy. In formal philosophy it is the study referred to as "Epistemology." The study of Epistemology addresses the question, "How do I know that I know?" It includes "What can I be sure is true? On what basis can I logically claim that a statement is true?"

Tragically, too few people ever stop to ask, "What can I be sure is true?" or seek an answer that can stand the test of examination and experience. The answer to this question however, affects every element of our lives both now and for eternity. Jesus linked "truth" to both "way" and "life" in stating His own nature. (John 14:6) Even though men may not stop to ask the question, there is an implicit statement of what they believe to be the truth in most of their actions. We accept a view of what is true when we buy a product, (Is the advertisement truthful?) vote for a politician, (Did he tell the truth in his campaign promises?) follow the advice of a doctor, (Is he telling us the truth about our problem?) hear another say "I love you."

Most people and most Christians never stop to say "How do I know that I know?" They simply say, "I think this is true." The problem consists in the fact that our view of truth, developed unconsciously, may mistake error for truth and truth for error.

Our Climate as Respects Truth

Christianity has always lived in a climate that takes a hostile attitude toward the Christian view of truth. The church in its beginning shortly suffered persecution because Christians denied the existence of other gods. Because of this their world considered them atheists, and since the emperor claimed to be a deity their beliefs were treasonous. If they had allowed Jesus and Jehovah to join the pantheon as equals to the Roman gods, there would have been little problem.

We find the world still presents Christianity with a hostile environment. Modern thinkers attack Christianity at this point. They deny the existence of any absolute truth. They don't realize that the statement "There is no absolute truth." constitutes a statement of an absolute truth. This "absolute" is necessary to rejecting Biblical Christianity. If Christianity has absolute truth (the existence of God, a "faith once for all delivered to the saints (Jude 3) and a final outcome for men and the world) then they would logically have to accept it. This is something modern thinkers are determined they will not do.

Today, in this country, we don't have legal or criminal persecution of Christians because of Biblical absolutes, but many Christians suffer such persecution in other countries. We have, however, Christians excluded from faculties, the faith of students belittled, and a barrage of efforts in the various media rejecting as prejudice elements of Christian faith. Recently we have had a series of court cases concerning freedom of Christian conscience with regard in particular to homosexuality. These actions and attitudes express rejection of a Christian life style as ignorant, old-fashioned, intolerant etc.

Some of this rejection may well constitute a proof of faith, since the Christian view does not allow a Christian to accept the non-Christian lifestyle. In fact he or she is obligated to reject it. (Romans 12:2) The Christian must reject any lifestyle that rejects or violates Christian revelation of right and wrong.

The Nature of the Question

We need to understand that what we are seeking in this discussion is not a list of true statements. We are asking the following questions:

- What is the nature of truth? Is it relative, absolute or attainable?
- What do we mean when we use the word "*truth*?"
- What determines whether something is true or not?

Among secular thinkers the most popular modern view, Pragmatism, claims that "a statement is true if it works, that is, if it accomplishes its purpose." Dr. Jack Cottrell (n.d., p.13) offers an example. An officer tells a story, which never happened, about acts of heroism by a soldier to "psych up" his troops. According to this view, if this succeeds, then he has told the truth. This action succeeded in "psyching up" the troops. They fought better. It leaves open the question of what the utility of the approach would be in the future when the subordinates have discovered that the officer has used fiction. Would it then be "true" when it didn't work? Can both logically be true? The Christian would answer, "No, truth is true and cannot change." It can be misunderstood or only partially true, the situation can change, but the true part is always true.

A Theory of Truth for the Christian

Most people seem to naturally accept this later view of truth. It is the correspondence concept of truth. This states that "a statement is true if it corresponds to *reality*." (Cottrell, n.d. pp. 11. 12) This is also a view of truth that is assumed by the Scriptures. Paul in 1 Corinthians 15:5—7 and 14—17 implies this idea of truth when he lists those who saw Jesus after the resurrection. He then says that if this doesn't prove that the resurrection is a fact, then faith (in the fact of the resurrection, as well as in many other facts) is vain or void.

How Do We Know Something Is True?

We find the first evidence for the truth of an idea in *our experiences.* It is not uncommon to say "I *saw* it happen." Or we may have heard something that which causes us we believe that it happened. This may happen as a result of the information gained from any of the senses. For most people, this constitutes the strongest and best evidence for the truth of something. John in 1 John 1:1—3 cites this as a dependable source of truth.

The *testimony of others* constitutes the second most common source of what we assume is true. You should remember that all truth reached this way is based on faith. That sounds as if it might be theoretical and not practical, but it constitutes one of the most practical parts of our existence. We literally live by faith. We drive a car because we believe that it will safely take us to our destination. We take a pill based on faith that the doctor has prescribed the right drug and the pharmacist has correctly dispensed it. There are a lot of drugs that look alike and most of them are poisons, if used improperly. We get married on faith. We listen to teachers on faith. Most of our courts base their view of truth on this type of evidence.

This does not constitute blind faith, or foolish faith. Generally, wise people test the witnesses. Don't you often select your doctor or your auto mechanic based of the testimony of people you trust? John (1 John 4:1) directs Christians to "try the spirits." John orders Christians to test the words and life of the ones who come as witnesses to see if they are God's messengers.

We may also look for *other corroborative evidence.* This might come from reasoning based on other facts that we assume to be "true." Peter (1 Peter 3:15) indicates that truth for a Christian is also a result of reasoning.

Though the philosophers may attempt to question it, this is the basis for truth in our society, the courts, science, and everyday life.

The Problem of the Finite Man.

Probably the greatest problem in defining truth and escaping error is found in the fallibility of man. We are imperfect creatures. We make mistakes. We have barriers in our thinking which create problems.

Sometimes we lack the needed background. Consider the following list of problems as you ponder the problem of arriving at certainty.

- No person can know all things, or everything about even one thing.
- Our consciousness is confined in a single space. (our experience)
- Our mind operates in a moment of time. (now)
- All ideas are filtered by our fallible senses.
- We experience a practical certainty in many life situations. Generally we feel certain that the pump tells us correctly the amount of gas we put into our car. We trust the testimony of a fallible representative of a fallible government for its accuracy. So, even this depends on faith, but this faith is based on evidence.

The most critically important decisions (those in the realm of spirit) often have the least available evidence received through practical certainty. (the senses) The only solution is in a God who is infinite and reveals Himself. He is not bound as we are by an egocentric limitation. We then base our faith both on history and on a host of credible witnesses to His wisdom and truth.

What Truth is Important?

The Christian must also make decisions as to what truth is important. John in 1 John 1:1 indicates this contrast as to Christ in the change of tenses between the first "heard and seen," and the "beheld and handled." The first two appear in the untranslatable tense, the Greek perfect, which indicates something happened and is still important, and the last two are in the simple past tense. John clearly indicates that the first two are the more important.

Many truths, even Biblical ones, are incidental, but some are essential. I am including a suggested list of areas of B*iblical truth which fall in the essential* group. Essential truths are those needed for the following:

- salvation
- Christian maturity and growth
- Christian assurance and joy

- Biblical teaching concerning church administration and leadership
- the church that is the true church
- a **B**iblical view of God and Jesus
- the fact that Jesus is coming again

They all represent truth if they correspond with reality which in this case is the will of God. (You can find this author's views on most of these things in his book *Acts, Blueprint for the Church.* (King, 2016)

There are other essential truths, Biblically based, but not directly taught by Scripture. These truths include at least the following subject areas.

- a Biblical understanding of truth
- items in the polemic against liberalism (materialisms, pragmatism, relativism)
- evidence for the acceptance of the Bible as God's word
- acceptance of the New Testament's teaching and approved practice as the one pattern for the church and for its membership.

The criteria for selection of the essential core include at least the following

- essential for the sake of our own salvation.
- essential to determining the question of fellowship with believers
- essential for living as Christians

Biblical References to Truth

Truth is important in the teaching recorded in Scripture. It is inextricably tied to Jesus in such passages as John 1:14 where He is described as "full of grace and truth" and 1:17 where we are told that "grace and truth came by Jesus Christ." It is a term used to directly describe him in John 14:6 "I am the way the truth and the life." John describes doing the truth as coming to the light. (John 3:21) He further describes when it says "Ye shall know the truth and the truth shall make you free." (John 8:32) The worship of God is to be in "spirit and truth." (John 4:24) The teaching of The Holy Spirit is identified as truth when in John 14:17, 16:7, 13 Jesus promises that that Spirit will guide them into all truth. Jesus further emphasizes this in His statement (John 17:17) "Thy word is truth." The Gospel is identified as truth by such passages as Galatians 2:5, 14; Colossians 1:5; James 1:18.

How Then Does the Christian Regard Truth?

First, it is that which corresponds with reality as he can best see it. This includes his observations and the testimony of credible witnesses. In matters of religious faith, he regards truth as most clearly found in God's revelation, which he believes is amply supported by a host of credible witnesses. He sees truth as so much a part of the nature of both God and Jesus that they cannot speak anything other than the truth. He sees truth as an absolute necessity for his life as a Christian and for the life of the church. He understands that he finds truth in God's word as communicated through men whom God inspired.

In secular matters he is a discerning thinker who considers truth necessary to everyday living and looks for the most credible witnesses to support that truth, including his own senses. He often reserves judgment when he believes that he does not have sufficient information from credible sources to permit making a sound judgment.

CHAPTER 2

WHAT IS THE NATURE OF EXISTENCE TO THE CHRISTIAN?

will approach this subject through a series of questions. These questions are:

- What is real?
- From where did it come?
- Does it have a purpose?
- What changes and what does not?
- Is reality friendly or an enemy?
- What will happen to it?

What Is Real?

Webster's Third International Dictionary (unabridged) (Compton's p. 1890), after dealing with legal usage, in 2b defines "real" as "actually existing, occurring or present in fact: corresponding to actuality?" Various schools of thought differ in how they understand the definition.

The Monistic Idealist

This persuasion says, with Plato, that the idea is real, all else is reflection of that idea. The Berklian Idealist says that only mind is real. This means that all our problems are simply failures to think correctly. The most popular form of this is Christian Science.

The Monistic Materialist

This is the view that all things are matter. It is most popularly advocated by some teachers in Psychology. One of the most extreme thinkers in this view was B. F. Skinner, a Harvard professor, whose view asserted that all of personality and "mind" is simply the pattern of synaptic responses and that men will be what they are "programmed" to be. The names for this view include connectionism, behaviorism S-R psychology. Robert Beck (University of Minnesota professor and a member of my doctoral committee) in *Introduction to Philosophy* (Brightman, n.d.) criticizes this view as a blatant denial of an entire body of evidence, namely human experience. Skinner's view eliminates personal responsibility from any moral theory since men must do what they are "programmed" to do. Therefore, Hitler did nothing wrong, he only did what he had to do because he was programmed to do it.

The Dualist

This view holds that reality is made up of material things and immaterial ones. The immaterial ones may be called soul or spirit. The two kinds of reality interact with each other at various levels depending on the theory with which they are associated. Dualist thinkers have various theories on the importance of one or the other and how they interact.

The Typical Man on the Street

This person who does not consider himself a philosopher is usually a dualist. His dualism leans toward the materialist view in some ways. He believes that material things are real, usually consciously or unconsciously giving material things a bit more reality than non-material ones. He believes in mind, emotion and personality as immaterial. The immaterial things are, in his view, somewhat less well defined or certain.

The Christian

Christian theology requires belief in a special type of dualism. This view recognizes the reality of the material world. It includes the belief that the material world is the creation of God (Genesis 1:1, John 1:1—5, Colossians 1:15—17, Acts 17:24—26) through his Son, the Christ. It also recognizes the existence of a world of spirit. (John 1:4, 3:6, 4:24) This world of the spirit is the proper place for man to have his primary location. (Romans 8:1—17, especially verses 8 and 9) The writer of Hebrews (Hebrews 12:26—28) and John (Revelation 21:1) (1 John 2:17) make clear that the permanent things are of the world of the spirit, and the material world is temporary. We see this at the basic level when we note that though people change physically, they remain the same person. What should the Christian think about the issue? Two passages seem of particular importance. John 4:24 states that "God is a spirit." Therefore, the world of the spirit must be real. The second, Genesis 1:1 asserts that God created the material world *ex nihilo.* (out of nothing) God simply gave an order to bring each element into existence and it came into existence. It now exists in the form that we experience it. The Scriptures also say (2 Peter 3:10) that the physical (material) world is temporary and will end.

Where Did the World Come From?

This is a question as old as philosophy. The ancient Greeks, believing that everything had to be the result of a cause, stated that there had to be a "prime mover" or first cause. They did not have a strong identification of this "mover."

The Secular Scientist

Secular science and Christianity have major differences over how the world came into existence. Many scientists claim to believe that the universe is the result of chance. It just happened. They maintain that there were forces not now working, that helped produce the changes. These are dated far outside of recorded history. The world and its inhabitants evolved by chance from the most basic units. They usually are committed to the theory of evolution and of ages of time in which it is said to have operated. Darwin himself stated that he had no theory to account for 1) the origin of life or 2) the origin of intelligence. He seemed never to ask about the origin of space and matter. Most scientific studies involve some estimate of the probability that an event occurred by chance. For example, statistically the likelihood of ten successive throws of a coin all being "heads" is, using the binomial expansion, approximately 1 in 1295. Most psychological studies reject the "null" hypothesis (This states that the event happened by chance.) at $p < .05$ or $p < .01$. This means that the event would have happened by chance only one time in twenty events or one time in one hundred events. The secular theorist seems to fail to grasp the overwhelming evidence for rejecting the "null hypothesis" (It all happened by chance.) in such things as the genetic codes in genes which have all the characteristics of a language.

The Typical Man on the Street

Many or most of this group never take time to ask these questions. They simply accept the general view of the secular scientist or they don't bother themselves. If they have some type of religion, they typically attribute the existence of the world to their primary deity.

The Christian

So far as the ultimate origin of the universe, the Christian recognizes it must be eternal matter, or eternal spirit. We have evidence on the one hand that matter changes, but doesn't cease to exist. It may be turned into energy (atomic fission) and this energy we know from the Laws of Thermodynamics is also not diminished but dissipates. In general the material world seems to be "running down." As we experience our lives, we find that the most durable part of us, our personhood, remains rather constant though our physical bodies are always changing and being renewed. The evidence leads to the conclusion that matter is less durable than spirit.

This still does not answer the questions, "How did existence begin? Where did it all come from?" The Greek philosophers acknowledged the necessity of the existence of a "first cause" from which all existence came. The characteristics of creation seem at every turn to be by "intelligent design." There are similarities among the created things that indicate the work of the same intelligence. There are things that depend on others. Flowers must have the pollen sacks on the legs of bees to secure the pollen they need to flourish. Who can better be assumed to be that designer than God?

This God is a spirit. (John 4:24) The Christian sees the origin of the universe in the work of this spirit. Genesis 1:1 says "in beginning God created." [In the Hebrew and Greek texts Moses in Genesis 1:1 and John in John 1:1 and 1 John 1:1 do not use "the" with "beginning."] The Christian definition of God to some extent is "the one with no beginning." Acts 17:24, Ephesians 3:9, Colossians. 1:16, 3:10, 1 Timothy 4:3 and Revelation 4:11 identify God as the creator of all things." Hebrews 1:10 states that God did the work of creation and verses 11 and 12 indicate that the physical world will be discarded by the One who created it.

Does the Universe Have a Purpose?

This question implies two questions. First, what is the purpose it now serves? Second, is it moving toward some conceived end?

The Secular Thinker

The advocate of evolution assumes that the world has the purpose of producing more complex, intelligent, and powerful creatures. This contends that there is an upward direction in development. Some thinkers, such as Arnold Toynbee, believe that the world is simply going around in circles. This is termed the "squirrel cage" notion of human progress. Probably the most popular view is that coming out of the thinking of such thinkers as William James and John Dewey. It holds that the only purpose of change (progress with no direction) is more change.

Although it is not a theory as to purpose, less optimistic secular thinkers hold that the end of change will be disaster. The Malthusian Theorem holds that the population of the world will outrun its food supply. The environmentalist often forecasts disaster unless major changes occur. The physicist sees the world as "running down." The astronomer sees the possibly of cosmic collision ending all human existence.

The Christian

The Christian believes that purpose exists for the world. This brings us to a division of philosophy called Teleology, which deals with the question of purpose in existence. Beck and Brightman. in *An Introduction to Philosophy* (Brightman, 1951, pp 226—250) deal with this issue. Other scholars have similar viewpoints. Their arguments for purpose usually include at least six assertions. Summarized below are the assertions which are generally as follows:

- Everything in creation seems to serve some purpose. This seems to indicate a plan. Some birds live by disposing of dead bodies. Others keep the insect population from destroying the world of plants. Honey bees are equipped with pollen sacs to cross-fertilize flowers. People are equipped with five senses, each serving a purpose.
- The "fittest" have larger survival rates. Their availability serves the purpose of strengthening the species. .
- Human beings behave according to pre-conceived purpose.
- Man's efforts in seeking beauty and truth indicate purpose.
- The fact that the mind plans and controls action indicates a purpose. This purpose may relate to the purpose of God, the ultimate mind.
- Law implies purpose. Human law intends to maintain order. Natural law exists to make things work. Light works to provide information. Sometimes darkness promotes repose and re-building.

We find this same pattern of purpose for each thing in the Bible. First, there is purpose for events in the period before sin. Statements such as the following indicate purpose. Genesis 1:26— 28 indicates that the physical world was created in order that man might be the ruler of a domain. Genesis 1:29 indicates that the physical world was given to provide mankind with food. Genesis 2:15 indicates that man was created to tend the earth. Genesis 2:8, 9 indicates that the world was given as a home for human society. Both Genesis 2:18, 24 and 1 Corinthian 11:9 indicate that woman was created for a purpose, "a help suited to him." (This is my translation.) Genesis 2:16, 17 indicates that God created the world as a place of moral choice so that mankind might be righteous, not merely innocent. Genesis 3:8 indicates that God created the garden as a place for companionship between man and Himself.

Scripture provides more information about the purpose of the creation of man. The Bible clearly indicates the following. Isaiah 43:7 says that man was created for God's glory. In Ephesians 2:10 we have the statement that we are created for good works. God's purpose was to create a family of brothers. (Romans 8:29) This has a number of elements in it as indicated in 1 Peter 2:9, including an elect race, a royal priesthood, a holy nation, a people for God's own possession. On a personal level Genesis 12:2 indicates that Abram was intended to serve a purpose. The Jew views the last line, "be thou a blessing," as a command. These examples make it clear that every Christian is a person who has been born for a purpose.

What Changes and What Does Not?

The Secular Thinker

Popular modern thought tells us, "The only thing that is sure is change." This view would imply that everything changes. It is certainly true that technology changes. In my lifetime I have seen mathematical devices change almost from the abacus to the hand held computer and this change is so fast that one source says a computer becomes obsolete in seventeen days.

We know that social change continues. When I was 15 years old, some frequently used words were not allowed in moving pictures and we correctly called "becoming sexual active," "fornication" and no moral person would consider it. There were a few "trial marriage" advocates, but not the open practice (We called it "shacking up.") so frequently practiced today. Morally it was dishonorable. We expected a good preacher to have a good deal to say about sin, repentance and hell fire. How often do you hear these extensively discussed in the pulpit today?

The Christian's View

The Christian recognizes that things change. This includes the whole world of technology and much of history. His question, however, is "Are there things that do not change and if so, what are they?"

Thinking of these changes we note that Jean-Baptiste Alphonse Kerr, a French philosopher contended that "The more things change the more they remain the same." (Rice, 2017) A considerable argument can be made for his viewpoint. Wars are still fought over the same issues. People love, hate, have children, are jealous, just as they did four thousand years ago. Right and wrong (sin) as Biblically defined has not changed. God has not changed. James (James 1:17) states emphatically that God cannot change. Hebrews 1:10 — 12 says "Thou Lord, in the beginning didst lay the foundations of the earth, and the heavens are the work of thy hands: 11) They shall perish; but thou continuest; And they shall wax old as doth a garment; 12) And as a mantle shalt thou roll them up, As a garment, and they shall be changed; but thou art the same and thy years shall not fail." It is interesting that when the Greek is literally translated, the last half of Matthew 28:20 reads, "I with you am all the days until the completion of the age." (My translation) The "I" is emphatic. Note the tense is present, not future. Jesus as God stands outside time. Anything that stands outside of time has no "room" to change. This does not deny that the body of Jesus changed.

Jesus says, "I go to prepare a place for you." (John 14:2, 3) Peter in 2 Peter 3:13 promises a new heave and a new earth. Hebrews 12:27, 28 speaks of things that cannot be shaken, that are eternal.

The law of thermodynamics states that "Heat is always moving to where there is none and so dissipating. " This implies a universe that is "winding down". We know the sun is a dying star, stars disappear, "black holes" drawing in astronomical bodies exist, etc. Thus the material world is temporary, but the spiritual one "cannot be shaken." It will endure beyond time. Revelation describes (perhaps symbolically) this new earth in chapters twenty one and twenty two.

The Christian also looks forward to tremendous changes in his state when he dies. Second Corinthians 5:1—10 describes these changes. First

Corinthians 15:40—54 give additional information concerning these changes. The book of revelation in symbolic language adds information concerning the changes that have occurred and will occur.

Is the World: Friendly, Indifferent, or an Enemy?

The Secular Thinker

The secularist gives no clear answer. He will probably say that the creation is indifferent. He may, with some "new-age" thinkers, consider it almost a god to be worshiped, and use such phrases as "mother earth."

The Typical Man on the Street

Most of these people will probably not consider the question. It is one of those things that "theorists" talk about, but makes little obvious difference in daily life. He will see in storms an unfriendly world, but in much of nature a friendly one. Such things as the ocean will be friendly as a source of transportation and recreation, but unfriendly as having some serious dangers.

The Christian

The account in Genesis 2:8—10 indicates that the creation originally was very friendly. It still retains some of these positive elements. It provides beauty, food, fuel, etc. The "earth" movement emphasizes this. It became less friendly "for thy sake." (Genesis 3:17—19) God saw this as necessary when man sinned. This caused the creation itself to be an imprisoned creation longing to be freed. (Romans 8:21—23) Therefore, it is friendly but bound to fulfill the will of the Creator in disciplining mankind. Since God is its creator, the creation must be respected. (Hebrews 12:18—29. especially Verse 29)

*What Will Happen to the World? What Is the
End of Existence, If There Is One?*

These questions involve two issues. First, what will happen to the world? Second, what happens to the spirit (personality, soul) in man?

The Future of the Physical World

The Secular Thinker

This group gives little thought to this issue. He will know that the law of thermodynamics states that "Heat is always moving to where there is none and so dissipating. " This implies a universe that is "winding down." We know the sun is a dying star, that stars burn out, that "black holes" exist etc. This would indicate that existence will end. They are little concerned with this since they assume it will not occur in the next several million years. Some environmentalists and some astronomers assume that the world as we know it will become uninhabitable because of environmental changes, or by a collision of the world and some other object in space.

The Christian

Second Peter 3:7, 10—13 tells us that this creation will be followed by new heavens and earth. Verse 13 and also Revelation 21:1, 5 reflect this fact. Hebrews 12:26, 27 presents the same message. Paul (Romans 8:20—22) looks to the time when no longer will the "whole creation growneth and travaileth" but will be "delivered from the bondage of corruption into the glory of the children God." This indicates not just the destruction of the known world, but that God will replace it with a new and better one.

The Future of the Individual

The Secular Thinker

People in our experience always die, except, if you accept the Biblical accounts, Enoch and Elijah. Secularists consider these Biblical stories myths. The secularist generally will hold that their own existence will end at death. The view which is popular in public education advocates the assumptions in *Charlotte's Web*. (White, 2006) In it the spider, Charlotte, weaves a web with "some pig" in it that keeps the farmer from slaughtering the pig. When the spider dies it says "Charlotte lives on in her children." (Many public educators think this is the best answer for children's questions concerning death.) I have seen some fiction in which church members advocate a view that "we live on in our children." Near the time of his debate with Robert Owen, Alexander Campbell, who greatly admired Owen, was with Owen observing some of Campbell's prize cattle. Owen held a view much like that in *Charlotte's Webb*. Campbell remarked, "I can't believe that your life is the same as those cattle." (Richardson, 1879) Actually, this view leaves the question unanswered if man is more than a beast and does not simply cease to exist at death. The persistence of "self" though the body changes seems to deny that the end of physical existence, is also the end of personality.

The Christian

This question has two answers, one *for the Christian*, the other for the one who is outside of God's redemption. As respects His redeemed children, 1 Thessalonians 4:16—18 tells us that the dead will rise, they will join those Christians that remain and will always be with the Lord. Christians believe that this will be with Jesus in a place which He will have prepared. (John 14:1—4) The word translated "mansions" or "rooms" is actually the Greek word for "dwelling places." In 1 Corinthians 15:35—54, Paul describes the change after death for the redeemed. At that time the redeemed will "put on" incorruption and immortality. (1 Corinthians 15:51—54) Until then, only Christ (God) has immortality. (1 Timothy 6:16.) As to the time before the second coming of Christ, it is clear from 1 Samuel 28:8—19 that, as in the case of Samuel, there is continuing conscious existence after death. Second Corinthians 5:1—10 reinforces this assurance, but with a warning.

The more troubling side of the question is "What is the *fate of the unredeemed*?" Jesus in the Sermon on the Mount gives a very basic contrast in Mathew 7:13, 14. His followers' enter a "narrow gate" and follow a "straightened" way that leads to life. Others would take a "broad" way that leads to destruction. The Greek word for destruction used here is defined by Thayer as "put out of the way entirely, abolish, put an end to, ruin, destroy. " (Thayer, 1886) It is very clear that (Matthew 13:49, 50) those who are not among the redeemed will be cast into a furnace of fire with weeping and gnashing of teeth. Luke 12:46—48 indicates a differential in punishment of the lost depending on the nature of their sin. The traditional view of the Roman church is that all the lost will suffer eternal torment. (Some, though saved, must suffer in purgatory for their misdeeds.) The constant contrast in Scripture of life and death as the difference in fate for the saved and the lost, causes some to doubt the traditional view which includes eternal life for *both groups* one in bliss and one in torment. This constant contrast of life for the redeemed and death for the lost along with the use of the Greek word for destruction has led some thinkers (Ashley Johnson (1915) and Russell Boatman (1980) for example) to see a time of torment in proportion to the evil done followed by the penalty for rejection of God which is extinction. They find a parallel in the physical world where in death the body that dies no longer has feeling, but returns to the elements from which it came.

The Scripture lists some persons who will go to this Gehenna or place of fire and punishment. They include (1 Corinthians 6:9, 10) fornicators, idolaters, adulterers, effeminate, abusers of themselves with men (homosexuals), thieves, the covetous, drunkards, revilers, extortioners. Paul seems to add to that list (1 Timothy 1:9, 10) murderers of parents, man stealers, liars, false swearers, those who do not teach sound doctrine. Jesus affirms some of these in such passages as John 8:44. We have a glimpse into this place in Luke 16:23, 24, and 28.

The attitudes of the Christian toward those who are lost should express obedience to the command that we love one-another. First John 5:16 clearly indicates that the Christian should pray for the lost. James reinforces this in James 5:16—20. First Corinthians 5:1—5 clearly indicates that the church cannot tolerate these immoralities, but 2 Corinthians 2:5—8 indicates that the repentant sinner must be received in love. So long as the person is living he has the assurance of God's forgiveness if he sincerely repents. This is stated in 2 Peter 3:9, and Revelation 22:17 and the principle is applied in Acts 2:38, Acts 3:19 and elsewhere.

A Christian View (Summary)

1. The Christian sees his world as a good gift of God, which must be respected both by caring for it and avoiding the dangers included in natural processes.
2. The Christian sees the world as a temporary place to be replaced by a new and better one.

3. The Christian sees the world as having a purpose given by God, and moving toward the fulfillment of His purposes.

4. The Christian sees the world as a place in which the enduring realities are spirit and material things are temporary materials to be used to support and assist the spiritual realities.

5. The Christian sees himself as a person with freedom of decision, who must make changes to conform to the purposes of the creator, but he/she sees these changes as tremendously to his/her benefit.

CHAPTER 3

AXIOLOGY: ETHICS AND AESTHETICS

*A*xiology is that division of philosophy that deals with values. It is usually divided into two areas, ethics and aesthetics. The first, ethics, seeks to determine what is right and wrong. The second seeks to determine what is good and beautiful.

The More Important Question, "What is Right and Wrong?"

Secular Human Ethics

I have an extreme statement of this view but cannot at this point document it, so I will paraphrase the statement. The view states that traditional moral commitments based on supernatural origins (Bible) are some of the most repressive forces faced by the natural needs of humanity. It goes on to classify them as therefore immoral because they encourage illusions about heaven and hell, and tend to deny or resist natural and necessary human values. That writer could find no acceptable basis for final conclusions as to right and wrong. This raises such questions as whether Stalin, Hitler, and Mao are guilty of any wrong-doing. With no ultimate source of right and wrong, why should men obey any standard?

Some call for the use of reason and experience as a moral guide. This may be an expression of Pragmatism. (If it works, it is right.) We mentioned this view in our discussion of the basis for truth. On the other hand, reason and experience for many lead to acceptance of Biblical teaching as to right and wrong.

Others make right and wrong simple conformity to the prevailing social standard. Those who advocate evolution based on an evolution of constant improvement would include this as part of that improvement. As a rather naïve graduate student at the University of Pittsburgh, I was asked to agree or disagree with the statement that "Jesus was crucified because he had been immoral." I asked the professor, John Harbaugh, what he meant by "immoral." His reply was "I was trying to find out what you mean by immoral." I am not sure that he explained, but I now see that if the prevailing social standards are the criteria for morality, then the statement was true.

Others advocate an ethics that is relative to the situation. Moral behavior is personal, so a given behavior might be moral for one person and not for another. It also may be related to the occasion, with a behavior being moral at one time and not at another. One of the more popular advocates of this view discusses the issue in *Situation Ethics – The New Morality*. (Fletcher, 1966) His general view is that the situation determines what is right or wrong based on objective facts or circumstance. The moral person must decide, based on the circumstances, what constitutes the most beneficial course available.

The humanist finds it difficult to establish a basic ethic theory. Humanists are aware of the logical inconsistencies and the dangers of ethical relativism, consequently their ethical assertions are necessarily vague. Their ethical theories are an effort to avoid recognizing a supernaturally determined moral order. Where it is possible they look for a biologically determined ethic. This has produced the view that homosexuality is biologically determined from birth, and now some are seeking a biological source for pedophilia and incest.

None of these views recognize any independent authority for ethics and morals. With no objective standard this leaves morality and ethics as merely conflicting opinions. The only alternative to divine revelation of morality is personal preference.

Christian Biblical Ethics

Christian ethics is inseparable from theology because it reflects the nature of God. Some things are harmonious with His character, some in conflict with His nature. His expressions of His will for His creation reflect His own nature. Instead of the changing whims of the relativist, men know the moral order though both general and special revelation.

A Morality That Even Controls God

Although the statement concerning God is true, there appears to be morality to which God, in turn, submits. Abraham refers to this when in Genesis 18:25 he asks, "Shall not the judge of all the earth do *krisin* (justice, right action)?" (*The Septuagint*) The Greeks said "no" and their gods were morally worse than humans. The answer here must be "yes." Therefore God is bound by an ethical standard. Hebrews 6:18 states that "It is impossible for God lie." His very nature binds Him to that which is true.

The Central and Controlling Principal

The Principal Defined

John in 1 John 4:16 states that "God is *agapee*." Most translate this as "God is love," but our English word "love" is not the same as the Greek word *agapee*. Theologians have spent countless volumes in "theologizing" this word. If their complex definitions correctly define the word, the Christian life becomes practically impossible. For men to be able to be Christians, the definition must be so simple and direct that "the wayfaring men, though fools, shall not err therein." (Isaiah 35:8) The lexicons do not usually give a simple definition. From them I have this definition, "a*gapee* constitutes the decision to value, esteem, feel or manifest generous concern for, be faithful to, set store upon, be devoted to the best interest of the one loved."

Furthermore, since it is commanded it must be something you can chose to do or chose not to do. You do not "fall into" *agapee*. This Greek word constitutes the central command of the two great commands on which the law rests (Matthew 22:37—39, Mark 12:30, 31, Luke 10:27, John 15:12, Galatians 5:14) and which are now the "law of our King" or the royal law (James 2:8) of Christians. God is one who has this *agapee* for man, and commands that it be returned and be directed to other men. *The best test* of right and wrong then, is the interaction within the situation of these two closely related commands.

Right and wrong depend in part on the nature of God, just discussed, and upon obedience to the commands which God makes, since these express and are the result of His nature. This is summed up in 1 John 5:1—3. As we come to know Him, we also come to know what is right and wrong. The fact that God made man in His own image and likeness makes it very clear that we are only doing "right" when we reflect His image by being as nearly like Him as is possible and proper for us. God makes His commands known to us thorough natural and special revelation.

Natural Revelation of Right and Wrong

Through the structure and operation of the world God makes known His will. This is in the form of "practical" morality. I mean by that term that God expects us to understand His creation and live in such a way as to not injure it or be injured by it. He implied this when he gave Adam and Eve the care of the garden. He has incorporated punishments when we fail to observe His law in nature.

Special Revelation of Right and Wrong

Commands Before Moses

God revealed right and wrong before He gave a law through Moses. Cain knew he had sinned when he killed Able. We see sin clearly known in the ethical situation at the time of Noah, (Genesis 6:1—8) and in the actions later of Noah and Ham. (Genesis 9:20—25) Pharaoh and Abram knew that adultery was wrong. Judah knew the law of the Levirate right of a widow. Shechem knew that rape was wrong. Simeon and Levi knew that they did wrong in their revenge. Rebecca and Jacob knew that they did wrong in deceiving Isaac. Circumcision became law for Abraham's family long before Moses. The duty of erecting altars and sacrifice is present throughout, though we have no record of a command for them. We don't know all of the provisions of God's law before Moses since we have no written record, nor do we know how it was communicated, but we know that every social group of mankind has known that some things were wrong. Paul in Romans 2:12 — 15 indicates that all the nations knew a law of right and wrong. All of this may have been handed down from Eden.

Commands Through Moses and the Law

Special revelation gives us a further presentation of God's teaching concerning right and wrong. The Law of Moses forms the first formal recorded record of God's view of right and wrong. This came by direct special revelation. In Exodus 20 3—17 we have the most reverenced of these commands, the "Ten Commandments." (They are called the Decalogue. (*deka* – 10, *logoi* – words) Jews consider them, not as commandments but "the ten words." (The words are those that define a Godly man.) Though very popular as a basis for law the New Testament makes it clear that The Law of Moses was not given for Christians and so cannot operate as our law but was taken away by the cross. (Colossians 2:14) (The major theme in both Galatians and Hebrews is that the Law of Moses has been replaced.) In 2 Corinthians 3:3 Paul clearly indicates that the Ten Commandments have been replaced. In fact Paul indicated the inferiority of the law in Galatians 3:24, 25 when he called it a *paidagoagos*. (*pais* boy, *agagos* leader) The term describes a decrepit servant given the job of taking the boy to school wiping his nose, seeing he was properly clothed, cleaning his slate, carrying his books. The *paidagogos* was not a "tutor" as some translators translate be word. He never taught the boy anything. The comparison is to the *didaskalos* who sat on a throne with the boys at his feet with a slave behind him who had the duty to chastise with rods any boy who didn't have his lesson. This relationship is represented in some of the ancient art. (See Cubberly, 1948) Paul (Galatians 3:13) describes the Law as a curse. Peter in Acts 15:10 describes it as a yoke that "neither or fathers nor we were able to bear." This law often gives instruction to be used in judging how to express love, but has no jurisdiction over us. The conclusion is that though the law defined sin, it is no longer a document having jurisdiction, though it may give guidance in applying the commandments of Christ.

Commands in the New Testament

New Testament commands are best expressed in the discussion we have above of the relation of the nature of God and right and wrong. The summary of the two basic principles in Christ's law appears there. All must be interpreted in the light of those commands, to have *agapee* for God and neighbors.

The details of the life of the one obeying the two great commands appears in the New Testament. Jesus in the Sermon on the Mount (Matthew 5—7) commends meekness (5:5), hungering for righteousness (5:6), mercy (5:7), peacemaking (5:9), serving as salt and light for the world (5:13—16), controlling anger (5:23), taking responsibility for reconciliation (5:23—26), having no desire for another man's wife (5:27, 28), rejecting divorce as an option (5:31, 32), rejecting swearing as wrong (5:33—37), seeking revenge as wrong (5:38, 39), loving your enemies (5:43—47), practicing charity in humility (secrecy) (6:1—4), privacy in prayer (6;5—8). He gives a model for prayer in Matthew 6:9—15. This listing is not complete. The Christian should study the life and teaching of Jesus for examples and instruction as to how He wishes the Christian to live. I note one strange flaw in most of the "Christian Doctrine" books. I find very few that attempt any genuine mastery of what the Teacher taught. (I am beginning the process of an effort to "fill the gap" with a "Christ centered" Christian Doctrine book.)

Christ here also gives directions for managing life. He indicates (Matthew 6:19) what your most valuable things should be. He urges us (Matthew 6:25) to trust God, and not be anxious. He warns us (Matthew 7:1) not to judge others. He urges us (Matthew 7:7) to have a good prayer life. The following statements appear to be conclusions from this discussion.

- The supreme test of ethical behavior is to imitate Jesus. Matthew 16:24—26 indicates that this imitation of Jesus is an absolute essential. This implies that we must get to know Jesus extremely well. This fellowship with Jesus forms the basis of our fellowship with Christians. (1 John 1:7) It also causes us to recognize sin in ourselves. (1 John. 1:10)

- The scriptures bind us to obey human law so long as it does not prevent us from obeying God's law. (Romans 13:1)

First John 4:7, 12 shows that *agapee* is central to our relation with others. It is also central to God's nature. (1 John 4:8) John ties this to an obedience to His commandments which are not burdensome. (1 John 5:1—3) If we love God we will seek to do his commandments.

How Do We Decide What Is Right and Wrong?

We need some principles which will enable us to determine whether actions are right or wrong. We need a way of determining (testing) what is the "will of the one living God, that which *is* ethically right, acceptable, and complete." (My translation) (Romans 12:2) Paul in the first part of the verse gives the means to accomplishing this. He indicates that first, we must not be "pushed into the mold" of this age and second, we must be transformed by renewing our minds. This teaches that our procedure should be something like the following.

First, we must not be "pushed into the mold" of this age. We need to ask how much the world is pressuring us in a particular direction and be prepared to resist that pressure. Many things assumed to be God's commandments are not supported by scripture. We must not demand of ourselves obedience to something not stated in Scripture by either precept or approved precedent. Some things forbidden in scriptures are often excused by the culture or even by religious leaders. Some of those pressures include the following:

- There is pressure from what the world around us thinks is right and best.
- There is pressure from the history of our culture.
- There is pressure from the family.
- There is pressure from within. We tend to want to keep the things we have assumed.
- There is pressure to justify behaviors which we prefer.
- There is pressure to maintain the thing to which we are accustomed.

- There is even pressure from a conscience which has not been taught by the renewed mind.

Second, Paul says that this is accomplished by renewing the mind. The purpose of this renewing is to "test what the will of God is." (Romans 12:2) The word renewing (*anakainosei*) comes from the word meaning a new kind. If it were simply different it would be a form of *neos*. This must be done with an open mind to listen, and with the best of our intellect "turned on." We are not to look for a book of rules. God in His wisdom did not give us a law book. The Code of Common Law of Kentucky contains many volumes.

How do you accomplish this "renewing?" How does The Holy Spirit operate on our spirits? The only certain way our minds are renewed is through hearing with faith. (Galatians 3:2) What does Paul include in that which the person should hear? Where does the Holy Spirit speak clearly to all men? We have God speaking the same words to all men only in the written Word. This would mean that the new kind of mind comes from study of the written Word. Therefore, we study the revelation given to "renew our minds." This must be done with an open mind to listen, and with the use of the best of our intellectual abilities.

What does the written word say about this? First, there is a rather broad statement by Paul when he says, (1 Corinthians 6:12) "All things are lawful for me; but not all things are expedient. All things are lawful for me; but I will not be brought under the power of any." Paul in 1 Corinthians 10:23, 24 repeats the statement down through the second "lawful" but adds instead of the statement about authority "but not all things edify. Let no man seek is own, but each his neighbor's good." All of the verbs in both passages are present tense which indicates continuing on-going action, so Paul is indicating that this must be the pattern of life of the Christian. The Greek "all" is never absolute, but means all within a defined group of things.

What is that defined group of things? Paul has indicated that even among "lawful" things there are things which the Christian should not practice. He says in 1 Corinthians 6:12 that he would not be brought under the power of any. Therefore, even among the lawful there are things that might enslave us and must be avoided. In 1 Corinthians 10:23 the second passage he says "not all edify" and Verse 24 he orders that each man seek his neighbor's good, not his own. This then eliminates any selfish actions and restricts motives to those that build up the life of the church.

Paul's teaching goes back to the two great commandments, and the central place of *agape* in obedience to God. What principles further define the correct decisions as to right and wrong?

First, we must recognize that God is the ultimate source of authority, yet in some sense morality is even above Him.

Second, we must accept the authority of His special revelation. Much of this is classified in Scripture as "mystery" but in Scripture the word mystery does *not* refer to the unknown, but to that which can only be known as God reveals it, for example note Jesus statement to Peter. (Matthew 16:17) These come to us by His special revelation. The Old Testament has moral absolutes given as a *paidigogos*. As we noted before the *paidagoas* (meaning "boy leader") was a servant given the job of taking the boy to school but who never taught the boy anything important. The comparison is to Christ as the *didaskalos* who sat on a throne with the boys at his feet. Yet, Paul says "If it had not been for the Law, I would not have known sin." (Romans 7:7) This statement may refer to Paul's former life as a Pharisee. On the other hand it is now the teaching of Christ that defines sin and right conduct.

The New Testament extends the moral absolutes. One of them is stated in Matthew 22:37—40. All the law and the prophets depend (have their base in and are obeyed if these are obeyed) on these two commandments. The New Testament elaborates these in such passages as the Sermon on the Mount. (Matthew 5—7) The supreme test of ethical behavior is to imitate Jesus. (Matthew 16:24—26) This implies that we must get to know Jesus extremely well. The Scriptures bind us to obey human law so long as it does not prevent us from obeying God's law. (Romans 13:1) First John 4:7, 12 makes love *(agapee)* central to our relation with others. It is central to God's nature. (1 John 4:8) This is tied to obedience to His commandments which are not burdensome. (1 John 5:1—3)

Third, we have to "watch our back" to see that in deciding in one direction we don't fail to take into account another teaching. This usually means that we need the fellowship of a number of other Christians whom we trust to help us make those decisions. If we had Biblical elders (shepherd/teachers in Ephesians 4:11), this might be a partial solution, but even they can be wrong. In this context, (Matthew 7:1) the Scriptures caution us not to condemn someone who sincerely disagrees with us.

Fourth we may look for a harmony with the natural order of things. This is a much more tenuous avenue to truth. It is sometimes termed general revelation. Since it is highly dependent on individual judgment it cannot be forced on the one who disagrees.

Believing that something is "right" does not obligate you to practice it. Conditioning factors might include:

- Would the act be an act of *agapee*?
- Would the act offend someone so as they might lose their faith?
- Would the act place obstacles before some area of your service?
- Would practicing it cause you to violate some other commandment?

The Second Question, "What is beautiful."

The scriptures have little to say at this point. First, what does the Old Testament say about beauty and what does it describe as beautiful? Beautiful appears nineteen times in the Old Testament. The Old Testament applies beautiful to women, (Genesis 29:17 to Rachel, Deuteronomy 21:11 to wives from conquered people, 2 Samuel 11:2 to Bathsheba, Esther 2:7 to Esther), the beloved one (Song of Solomon. 6:4) and her feet. (Song of Solomon 7:1) Other passages classifying things as "beautiful" include references to faces, (1 Samuel 16:12, and 25:3) everything (created?) in its time, (Ecclesiastes 3:11) the "branch of the Lord," (Isaiah 4:2) garments, (possibly spiritual) (Isaiah 52:1) the temple that had been burned, (Isaiah 64:11) of a flock which was their possession and would be taken away, (Jeremiah 13:20) of a rod that would be broken, (Jeremiah 48:17) figuratively of Israel and its crown (Ezekiel 16:12, 13) and of crowns on the heads of adulterous people. (Ezekiel 23:42)

Beauty occurs more frequently, appearing eight times in the historical books and forty-one times in the poetic and prophetic books. The following indicates some of the typical references. It appears first in Exodus 28:2 and 40 in reference to the beauty of the garments prepared for the priests. It appears as a reference to the beauty of holiness in 1 Chronicles 16:29, Psalms 29:2 and Psalms 96:9. It is used with reference to God in Psalms 90:17. There is a reference to beauty as vain in Proverbs

31:30. Proverbs 20:29 says the beauty of the old man is his gray head. Other translations use different expressions.

In the New Testament, "beautiful" appears in the English translations three times and one is a near quote of Isaiah 52:7, "the feet of them that bring good tidings and publish peace." This is the only place *naw-ow* "at home, pleasant, suitable, beautiful" appears in a translation as "beautiful." The LXX makes it from the same root as *horios*. The word *horios*, translated "beautiful" appears only Acts 3:2, 10 and Romans 10:15. It is defined by Moulton as "timely, seasonable, in prime, blooming, beautiful." Bromley (Kittle) notes that the root word is attached firmly to the idea of time. Because of the meaning of Romans 10:15, I tend to favor the idea of timely or convenient. Therefore the statement is that the feet of those that bring the gospel are "timely." My experience is that God seems to arrange at times for his messengers to appear at the time they are needed. This would make the reference to the gate of Jerusalem, the convenient gate, not the beautiful one. I know of no ancient description of the gate.

Summary Thought

The Bible doesn't give us a definition of beauty. In God's eyes, it appears to be related to the ethically good in a metaphorical sense, and in a literal sense to that which best reflects the intention He had in creation. Further, it seems clear that the results of sin are not beautiful.

It appears that God is interested in beauty and that the perfection of His intent and design constitutes the highest beauty.

CHAPTER 4

THE BIBLE IN A CHRISTIAN WORLD VIEW

*I*n the first chapter we discussed what Christians believe about truth. During that discussion we asserted that the Christian accepts the Bible as God's revelation to man, and therefore the content of it is revealed truth. Now we want to look specifically at this source of truth. In the process we seek to establish that the Bible is that truth, and therefore the authority in matters of Christian faith.

Required Characteristics:

What are the characteristics of the Bible which the Christian should believe to be true in order for it to have a proper place in his/her life? The Christian should believe that the Bible has at least the following characteristics.

The Bible Is a Uniquely Inspired Revelation.

The Christian must see the Bible as an *inspired revelation*. Inspiration of the Bible by God is an absolute essential to the place of the Bible in the life of the Christian. In John 16: 7 Jesus promised that He would send a *parakleetos* who "when He is come He will convict the world...guide you into all the truth." (John 16:8, 16:13) The translation "comforter" used by the KJV (The Bible, KJV) in my opinion is an unfortunate one. The word Christ used (*parakleetos)* means "1. One who pleads another's cause. 2. an intercessor... 3. in the widest sense a helper, succoror, aider, assistant..." (Thayer). In other words He fulfills all the functions a good friend might fill. In this case His most important function was (Verse 13) to guide the apostles into all truth. Any good interpretation of Scripture must ask who the words were spoken to and for what purpose, as well as who said them. In this case Jesus addressed the apostles to prepare them for their unique ministry. The promise is made to *no others*. He repeats the statement to the same people in Acts 1:8 in saying "You will receive power when the Holy Spirit is come upon you; and ye shall be my witnesses...." John 16:14 and 15 indicate a line of revelation from Father to Son to Holy Spirit. Therefore, the teaching of the Apostles becomes God speaking as He inspired them. In 2 Timothy 3:16 we have Scriptures referred to as *theopneustos* using a word which combines "God" and "breath." The word appears only here in the New Testament. Some press to translate it "God breathed" or "breathed by God". I prefer to translate it as "given by divine inspiration" since this it does not ascribe to God a function which requires lungs and a physical body. These Apostles then had that inspiration as they wrote. John 16:13—15 indicate that the Holy Spirit would say only what Jesus said and Jesus would say only what the Father had given Him. Therefore, the inspired statements of the Apostles are the statements of God.

What about Mark, Luke, James and Jude? The Apostles had the ability to impart miraculous gifts but only they had this power. (Acts 8:14—17) Paul lists the "gifts of the Spirit in 1 Corinthians 12:4—11. These include: 1) wisdom, 2) knowledge, 3) faith, 4) ability to heal, 5) working miracles, 6) prophecy, 7) discerning of spirits, 8) kinds of tongues and 9) interpretation of tongues. Numbers 1, 2, 3, 6, 7, and 9 have to do with knowing the truth as God reveals it. These writers had ample opportunity for the Apostles to lay their hands on them to give the needed gift (s). Therefore when these people died the gifts ceased as indicated in 1 Corinthians 13:9—10. No other writings have this kind of inspiration.

The Bible Has Authority.

The Christian also see the Bible as *having authority*. Jesus in Matthew 28:18 claimed all authority in heaven and in earth. Being God's revelation gives to the words of God (the Bible), those of Jesus, and those of the Holy Spirit (in the Bible) final and universal authority. Jesus recognized the authority of the Old Testament books. Mark (Mark 12:24) quotes Jesus who cites them as an authority. Jesus further says (John 10:35) that they are the word of God and cannot be broken. (made to contradict themselves) James 2:8 and 4:5—7 clearly indicate that this inspired writer considered them as having authority.

The Bible As We Have It (The Canon) is Complete and Authoritative.

Canonicity constitutes the third and final characteristic of the Christian's view of Scriptures. In 1 Corinthians 12: 8—10, Paul lists among the gifts of the spirit "the word of knowledge ....prophecy, and discerning of sprits." In 1 Corinthians 13:8 Paul says that prophecy, knowledge and tongues would be done away. He says 1 Corinthians 13:10 that this would happen when the complete thing (neuter, nominative, singular) had come. The article is in the substantive position, so "thing" is implied, and the word *teleion* means properly "brought to its end, finished, wanting nothing necessary to completeness, perfect." (Thayer) This is enforced by Jude's statement (Jude3) that "the faith (which) was "once for all delivered unto the saints." The only significant new thing in Christianity to be completed after Paul wrote these words is the New Testament. The special gifts of knowledge and discernment were given by the laying on of the hands of the Apostles. It is quite likely that people who had received these gifts lived well into the second century. In the first century it is clear that the writings which we have were given the status of inspired Scripture. The first listings of the books to be included were written in the middle of the second century. By 200 AD Origen listed all of our twenty seven books as inspired writings. In the next century we have a dozen lists of these books, representing writers from all parts of the known world. The children of those with the gifts given by laying on of the Apostle's hands could have known the writers who wrote the lists. (The simplest list I have found of the lists of books accepted as inspired during early church history is in *Lost Books of the Bible*, Table II, page 291ff.) (You might also consult the discussion by J. W. McGarvey.) (McGarvey, 1886) Only one book not in our New Testament was proposed as included, the Epistle of Barnabas. This was proposed by one writer in northern Italy and no one else. The early lists, at times, excluded Revelation; in fact the Council of Laodicea in 364 omits it. With this exception these twenty seven books and no others were accepted through-out the known world by the end of the third century. (The known world at that time by air-line distance extended about 6,000 miles. The distance by road was much greater and the most rapid travel was by horseback. In spite of this difficulty these and only these were accepted.) This acceptance of the same books by the church throughout the known world by the mid-second century could not have happened by chance. This requires that canonicity finds its base in the divinely given gifts provided the church by the Apostles until the New Testament could be written.

The Bible Also Has Unique Characteristics.

The Christian should also see the Bible as having other unique characteristics. *First* it has one Author, God through the Holy Spirit. *Second* it is a wonderful collection representing a number of different genres. *Third,* those who wrote for the books represent a number of different cultural backgrounds. *Fourth,* the work of writing spanned a period of about 1500 years. *Fifth,* the unity of the Bible is itself a miracle. The Author is God through The Holy Spirit and inspired men. Each of these wrote within his personal culture and abilities. *Finally,* textual criticism (the science of determining the statements written by the authors) has demonstrated that the New Testament is by far the best preserved of any ancient document.

How Should the Bible Be Used?

Since these characteristics apply to the Bible the Christian must consider it a book to be studied with care having a message to be understood, believed and obeyed. It must be handled correctly. (2 Timothy 2:15) Paul in the same epistle (2 Timothy 3:15—17) indicates that the Christian will consider it as 1) able to make you wise unto salvation, 2) profitable for reproof and correction of errors, 3) profitable to instruction in righteousness, (In a number of places, particularly in Paul's writings, *dikoosunee* may be better translated "justification" rather than "righteousness." See the Reece 1996 and Lard 1875.) 4) able to make the man of God "complete, furnished completely to every good work."

Therefore, the Christian must accept the Scriptures as the basic textbook for living and teaching Christianity. Jesus used them. (Luke 24:27, 32, 45) The Apostles used them. (Acts 17: 2, 3) The Bereans were commended for using them. (Acts 17:11) Apollos used them. (Acts 18:28) Timothy was told to use them in the passage just mentioned. (2 Timothy. 3:14, 15) Paul (Romans 15:4) describes them as written for our learning.

The Christian should consider them the true Word of God given once for all time. (Jude 3) This makes the Bible absolutely unique. It also places some limitations on its use. It must not be altered or added to in any way. This would deny its function. It must not be interpreted to support personal preference. Peter (2 Peter 1:20) prohibits any private (one's own, special) interpretation. He further indicates that those who "wrest" Scripture (use it to their own purposes) risk destruction. (2 Peter 3:16)

The Christian should make every effort to see that he attempts to consider all the Scriptures actually say, and avoid saying anything they do not say, so that he may make an educated Christian judgment where that is possible. He should make the best use possible of the principles of good Hermeneutics. This involves understanding a) the context in which the scriptures is written, b) the person writing or speaking, c) the persons spoken to, d) the purpose for which they are spoken, d) the grammar of the statement and e) the culture within which the statement is made. This is simply good Biblical interpretation. (Hermeneutics) You may want to review our introductory section on Hermeneutics.

A Christian should also be committed to five principles which are as follows. *First*, the Christian will speak where the scriptures speak. *Second*, he will be silent where the scriptures are silent. *Third*, he will regard some conclusions drawn from Scripture as possibly truly scriptural teaching, but as binding only on those who see them as being necessarily true. *Fourth*, he will not allow differences concerning the third classification to create divisions in the church or between Christian brethren. This is a paraphrase of Thomas Campbell. (Murch, p.46) *Fifth*, he will try to be aware of his own bias and its origin and minimize its impact on any conclusions drawn.

Attitudes Toward the Bible

There are some attitudes toward the Bible which the Christian should never take. These include at least the following:

- using it as a lucky charm
- considering it a book that he serves God by reading
- considering it a book of advice
- considering it a family heirloom
- considering it a book to be worshiped
- using it as a source of texts to prove one's own points

On the other hand, there are some very appropriate attitudes toward the Bible. These include at least the following: It is:

- a very valued possession
- the source I go to get answers for questions
- a comforter
- a source of inspiration
- an exhorter
- a source of guidance
- the source of the most important knowledge
- a source of facts to be believed, commands to be obeyed, warnings to be heeded and promises to be enjoyed.
- the primary source of ethical standards.
- a source of comfort and hope. (Romans 15:4)

Which Version of the Bible Should We Use?

What characteristics should the Christian require with regard to the translation he/she makes his primary version for study? My list of those characteristics may not be as complete as others but I believe it deals with all the essential elements.

I. *Accuracy*: It should faithfully present what the author was attempting to say within his culture and abilities. It should follow the best textual criticism in determining what has been written. As an English teacher, I believe that much of the meaning of a passage is dependent on the grammatical construction. For example many of the more recent translations and even the most recent Greek texts tear Ephesians 5:22 out of the paragraph, make it a separate sentence and paragraph and a command when it is actually a participle modifying the subject "you" of the command in verse 18. I also regret that the NASV (The Bible, NASV) in its introduction refuses any responsibility for translating the difference between the perfect (action in the past still having an important influence) and aorist (simple past tense) tenses. To me this denies the reader important elements in the message of Mathew 16:19; 18:18 and 1 John 1:1, for example, as well as many other passages. In the first two passages the KJV (Bible, KJV) and most others use two future tenses. The Greek has in each a future, then a perfect tense. The perfect tense indicates something that has happened in the past and is still having an important effect. This limits Peter and the Apostles to that which had been bound and was still bound in heaven.

It should be a translation in which the translator makes every effort to avoid the impact of any personal bias. Paraphrases leave a wide door open for this corruption. The translator must make personal judgments as what words best translate the Greek. The reader should, therefore, as far as possible, know the probable bias of the translator.

I maintain that accuracy requires, for example, that the translation report as accurately as possible exactly what the writer wrote. We may need to study the culture to understand some of these references, but this is our responsibility and is available.

The difference between a literal translation and both a "free" translation and a paraphrase is the same for both. The paraphrase is simply a more "free" translation. The writers of the translation simply deny responsibility for precise transfer of meaning and it becomes even more of a commentary than a translation. The "commentary" incorporates even more fully and perhaps more insidiously the preferences and bias of the writer.

II. *Utility*: Type size and legibility should be such that the reader can easily read it perhaps even in limited light. (This is a bit like the ADA legislation of the US congress.) The paper should be such that the person with limited ability can easily turn the pages. It should be in a form that is useable with economy even in difficult situations. .

III. *Clarity*: The language should be such that the usual (not ordinary – there are none) man can understand correctly. (Isaiah 35:8) Language does become outdated, but on the other hand the formal English even of the King James Version (a true scholarly classic though it has some bias and a number of obsolete expressions) has a durability and dignity that make it more useful.

There is a place for a translation that makes the Bible available to men of different languages, cultures, abilities, and age levels. This is a very difficult work if the translator is to have a clear loyalty to what the original writers actually wrote.

The first characteristic, accuracy, is the most important. Prefaces and annotations provide some safeguards. The ASV (The Bible, ASV) has many of them. If there are none, it may be that it is a weakness of the translation. Every translation should make alternate readings available to the reader. It is regrettable that few people give these much attention. Some other safeguards are 1) comparing the versions (A group translation is usually best.), 2) checking passages against other passages and 3) verifying the interpretation by a trusted commentary. (Remember, however, that a commentary is an opinion, and you need to "test the spirits to see if they be of God." (1 John 4:1) The test is whether they agree with Biblical revelation.)

Summary

The Christian considers the Bible as the voice of God speaking and inerrant in the documents actually produced by the inspired writers. He goes to the Bible to determine what is right and wrong. He goes to the Bible for the only authoritative teaching concerning how a man may be saved and what the practice and teaching of the church should be. He also goes to it to received comfort, encouragement, assurance, and strength. He goes to the Bible for instruction in how to live in the church, in his home, in his society, in his leisure, and in his work.

CHAPTER 5

WHAT KIND OF GOD DO YOU HAVE?

O penly atheism will not corrupt Christians. Opponents of Christianity seek to imply that God is not the center of things, that if He exists, judgment need not be based on recognition of this existence or any revelation of Him.

This book seeks to avoid a theology course, though theology is essential. We assume the understanding of the nature of the Bible as described in the previous section. We are not attempting to deal with Apologetics. That study will adequately indicate God's existence, and His revelation of Himself through the Bible. These things are assumed for the Christian. We are attempting to get at the view of God a Christian should have and which will be his guide to daily living.

God's Nature

Possibly the best Scriptural statement of the nature of God appears in Paul's speech on Mars Hill. (Acts 17:23—31) Only here, in the book of Acts, do we have record of a presentation of Christianity to a Gentile audience. Since we are in that group, it should be particularly pertinent. Paul describes God in a series of statements.

- He made the world and all things therein.
- He is Lord of heaven and earth.
- He does not dwell in temples made with hands.
- He is not served by men's hands.
- He needs nothing from us.
- He gives all life and breath; and all things.
- He made all nations.
- He determined the seasons of the nations. (rise, health, decline)
- He determined the bounds of the territories they held. (their habitation)
- He is not far from each of us.
- He wants men to seek after Him and find Him.
- "In Him we live and move and have our being."
- We are His offspring.
- He is forgiving. ("The times of ignorance therefore God overlooked.)
- He demands universal repentance from sin. ("Now He commandeth men that they should all everywhere repent.")
- He is just and will judge in righteousness.
- His righteousness and judgment are linked to their acceptance and obedience to Christ.
- He has given more than adequate reason for men to give that belief, acceptance and obedience. (v. 31)
- Some other characteristics of God include the following. He is eternal as to the past. (Genesis 1:1) His nature is a spirit. (John 4:24) He is ultimately ethically good and the only One who has that characteristic in an ultimate sense. (Matthew 19:17) He is unchangeable. (James 1:17) He must be reverenced. (Psalm. 19:1, Romans 1:20) His creation reveals Him. (Romans 1:20) He is the source of every good (ethically) and perfect (complete) gift. (James 1:17) He owns us and we must glorify Him in our bodies. (1 Corinthians 6:20)

His Nature as Revealed in Jesus

In John 14:9 Jesus said "he that hath seen me, hath seen the Father." He reveals His nature in Jesus. Matthew 11:27 adds that "...neither (is) anyone knowing the father except the Son and anyone to whom the Son might plan (desire, have purpose to) to reveal (Him)." (My translation) What does that tell us of Him as a person? Four inspired men each wrote accounts to tell us this, so what we say here is only a sketch and should be elaborated by every Christian as he studies the Gospels. These are a few of the things that we see in Jesus that help us see God.

He was Interested in Helping People.
He Loved (eegapeese) Them.

Jesus was very interested in the psychological well-being of people. He deals gently and courteously with those who question His commands. (Note his courtesy to John in Matthew 3:15, concerning John the immerser's protest.) He often sought to alleviate anxieties as indicated in the Sermon on the Mount. (Matthew 5:10—12, 17—20, 6:9—15, 19—21, 25—-34, 7:7—12, 7:24, 25) He sought to give peace and rest. (Matthew 11:28, 29 and John 14:1—3) His constant greeting was "be not afraid" (Mathew 14:27, Mark 5:36, 6:50, John 6:20), or "peace be with you." (Mark 5:34, Luke 2:14, 8:48, 24:36.) He shows great compassion for sinners. (John 8 and elsewhere) He had deep sympathy for our grief. (John 11:35) He loved children (Matthew 19:13—15, Luke 18:15—17, Mark 10:13—16) and both sought their happiness and wanted to be near them. He has great concern for the individual. (Matthew 18:13, 14) He wants his people to have joy. (John 15:11)

He was also concerned for the physical well-being of people. He was concerned for their physical comfort and safety. (Matthew 14:20, 31; 15:32) He was concerned for human suffering, healing all manner of suffering. (Matthew 4:23—25 and many other places) Even those outside his mission were given his help, such as the Canaanite woman in Matthew 15:22—28. (Also in Mark 7:24—30)

He Opposed the Bad and Hypocritical.

He clearly opposed evil, hypocrisy, and materialism. (Matthew 5 — 8) He rejected piety based on tradition and sought a piety based on service to others (Matthew 9:14-17) and obedience to a few simple commands of God. In Matthew 15:1—20 and Mark 7:1—25 He rebuked hypocrisy and ceremonialism in religion.

What Kind of People Did He Seek?

Jesus sought the service of simple, ordinary, even poor people, but the service was always for their best interest, not the service given a monarch or autocrat. (Matthew 5—8) He also sought people with a simple practical faith in Him. Examples include the centurion (Matthew 8:10) and the disciples on the sea. (Matthew 8:26) As a central part of his message and work He sought people who acknowledge their sin. (Matthew 9:11—-13)

He sought people who would develop a sincere faith. This might be as small as the mustard seed (Matthew 17:20, Luke 17:6) but He assured them of its power. He sought people who would come with the simple faith a child has in good parents. (Matthew 18:3—5, Luke 18:17) He also sought people who were willing to suffer for their faith (Matthew 10:34—39) even with persecution from the members of their own families.

By His example and His precept He taught caution in trusting men. (Matthew 10:16) He taught that His followers should expect persecution as a natural and rational result of following Him, (Matthew 10:17, 18) but He also taught that there was no need to fear (Matthew 10:28- 33) so long as they were faithful. He asks stewardship of blessings given. (Matthew 25:14 — 45) He taught thrift in His command that they gather up the fragments in order that nothing be lost after the five thousand men and their families had eaten from five biscuits and two sardines. (John 6:12)

His Own Dignity

He accepted worship. (Matthew 21: 9) He emphatically rejected desecration of the sacred. (Matthew 21:12, 13) He correctly considered His death and resurrection, even with its suffering, His greatest triumph. (John 17:1 – 5) He showed great dignity and restraint under persecution.

(Mark 15:3 — 5) He claimed all authority in heaven and on earth and gave commands for the lives of His followers. (Matthew 28:18—20)

His Personality

In social relations He accepted invitations, enjoyed social contacts and was a welcome guest at a wedding. (John 2:1—11) Evidentially He was no recluse. He seems to have had a sense of humor. My New Testament professor in college said that He never laughed. This is an argument from silence and logic says that such an argument as strong for as against the issue. It may have been that He laughed so much it just wasn't mentioned. I think that He had a sense of humor. His interview with Mary in this chapter of John seems to me to be teasing her, joking with her. Notice: 1) She turns to Him for help. Evidentially, she was confident that He would help. 2) He replies, "Woman...my hour is not yet come." 3) Then she turns to the servants and says "Whatsoever He saith unto you, do it." That is a strange reaction if she had just been rejected. I think there was twinkle in Jesus' eye and she knew that He was being humorous.

Mary's reaction on this occasion is another indication of a personality characteristic of Jesus. He was one you could depend on to help when help was needed. Confidence in Him was easy and very appropriate.

Men easily accepted Him as a leader. (Matthew 4:18—22) These men left their "gainful employment" to follow Him at a simple request. These men had known Him before and now chose freely to do this. It was not deterministic predestination.

He has little regard for human social barriers. (John 4) It was socially improper for Him to deal with a Samaritan and also perhaps even more socially unacceptable for Him to converse with a woman, much less a strange woman when He had no witnesses. He ate with those that His social group rejected and recruited one of them to work with Him. (Matthew 9:9-13) He touched the leper, (Matthew 8:2, 3) and allowed the woman accused of "many sins" to wash His feet with her tears, dry them with her hair and anoint them with kisses and perfume. (Luke 7:36—50)

There is no conflict between this and Paul's teaching in Romans 14:13—23, 1 Corinthians 10:23—33 and 1 Thessalonians 5:22. ("Go on holding yourself back from all *eidous* (form, appearance) of wickedness.") (My translation.) Paul clearly affirms Christian freedom, but made the issue whether the action might cause someone else to stumble.

Admittedly at times it is difficult to judge this issue. My brother- in- law went one night each week to bars in Saginaw, Michigan in a program called "night watch." The liberal ministry of the town didn't believe a conservative minister would dare to do it. He found opportunities for winning people to Christ he could have found in no other way. My minister friend would not enter a house unless he was sure that the woman's husband was there. If all facts were known both were right, but God does not leave us with simple situations. We have to act in faith.

He shows concern that people not be humiliated. (John 2:1—9; 12:5—8) He accepted the social outcastes. (Luke. 5:27— 32; 10:33—37) He forgives but includes the command that she "sin no more." (John. 8:11) He is preeminently good friend. (John 15:14, 15)

He recognizes sacrifice which may seem small to others (Mark 12:41—44) but should be evaluated in terms of the ability of the person to give.

He shows God as the father of the prodigal son, waiting, watching, welcoming. (Luke 15:20—24)

He repeatedly demonstrates (John 6:11, 12) that He could take little things and make great things of them. The five thousand who ate were filled indicating the abundance from what seems a very small food supply.

In practical situations He believes in avoiding waste. (John. 6:12) No service is beneath His dignity. (John 13:4—11)

He believed in vacations (Mark 6:31) but recognizes that there is another rest for the faithful. (Hebrews 4:8—11)

Jesus still recognizes the loss resulting from sin. The prodigal son (Luke 15:31) did not have another inheritance. The son could not forget the loss of the years to himself and his father. He could not undo the pain to his father even though it was forgiven. Jesus did not minimize the break in relations with his older brother.

His role in life was and is that of a teacher. (John 3:2, 20:16) Jesus is called *didaskalos* (teacher) about fifty times in the Gospels. Regrettably, the King James Version translates it as "master" meaning a school master, using a term that is obsolete in our day. The summary of His teaching in Matthew 5—8 demonstrates (subject to Matthew's understanding) a marvelous teacher who showed interest in His students. As a teacher He sought the simplest expression. He built on the previous knowledge and experience of His students. His material (again reflecting Matthew's summary) was well organized but easily comprehended. In other places He used the tools of the best teachers: illustration, figurative language, questions and answers, and demonstrations. His miracles fall into the last classification in that they demonstrate His power over every situation. Even in dealing with the Devil He demonstrates that temptations should be answered with God's word. (Matthew 4:1—11)

His Demands

His basic and fundamental requirement is that men believe, trust and obey Him. He states this in John 3:16, 17 and adds that He did not come to condemn but to save. He forgives but asks repentance. (John 8:11) He requires that we obey what James (2:8) calls the royal law (or law of our king) as to our fellowmen and the greatest commandment as regards God. Both of these required the kind of "love" called *agapee*. (This love is a commitment to do what we sincerely believe to be to the best interest of the object.) First, this relates to God then man. (Mark 12:29, 30) This is completely in harmony with His description of the judgment day and the requirement of stewardship of benefits given. (Matthew 25:37—46) First John 5:1—3 clearly states the requirement that men obey God's commands, but indicates that these are not "burdensome." (I prefer this word rather than the word "grievous." Both appear in the Lexicon.)

Our Relationship With Jesus

We have listed many of the characteristics of Jesus. Since Jesus said, "he that hath seen me hath seen the father" (John 14:9) we understand that these characterizes of Jesus are also characteristics of God. We have indicated above what a Christian should believe as to Jesus' nature in a number of situations. The additional belief concerning Christ which God requires of a Christian is to believe that Jesus is the eternal only begotten Son of God. (John 3:16, Matthew 16:15—17)

A Christian should also see Jesus as also his Elder Brother, his Lord, his High Priest, his Savior, and most importantly as concerns his way of life, his Teacher and Friend. (John 3:2. John 15:14, 15, John 13:13) Jesus was called and frequently called Himself "teacher." He sent His Holy Spirit to (John 14:26) "bring to your remembrance all that I said unto you. " This was a promise to the apostles. It becomes a promise to us as they through the written Scripture bring these things to us. He, then, is our Teacher in all that the Holy Spirit has caused inspired writers to write in Scripture.

Our Relation to God

In Acts 17:26—31, Paul indicate the elements in our actions necessary for a proper relation to God He includes these statements. We are God's offspring. He has set a day in which He will judge the world. His judgment will be in righteousness. The judgment will be by the man He ordained (Jesus), whom He raised from the dead.

We must remember that we are creatures; God is the creator. We are always utterly dependent on Him. We must not think of Him as impersonal, but rather as a personal being who loves (*agapao*) us and wants fellowship with us. We should believe that God is always with us, blessing, answering prayers, and showing Himself in nature and its forces in all types of expression. We must constantly be aware of the saving grace He has provided. We must conceive of Him as all that we have indicated concerning Jesus.

We must obey Christ's command to "be watching" (I realize that the emphatic force of this word had faded in common use in Jesus' day, but the idea is still there.) to see His daily presence in our lives. (Matthew 28:20) (The footnotes in the ASV (Bible, ASV) gives a literal translation of this verse as "all the days" unto "the consummation of the age. The "I" is emphatic.) We should be conscious of His presence especially when we read the Bible, or hear it taught.

How Does This Affect How We Live?

First, in the model prayer Jesus instructed His disciples to address God as "our Father." We live each day as His children, and He functions in all the ways of a good father. He offers Himself as our ever present guide, helper, friend, and protector. We should recognize that He is interested in the smallest details of our life and welcome Him as a loving friend. My wife taught me to see and practice the idea that He is interested in the smallest details. As a result when I misplace my glasses, I pray for His assistance in finding them and thank Him when I find them. *Second*, our love (*agapee*) for Him will cause us to obey His commandments. (1 John

5:3 and John 14:15) I translate the later verse as "If you are loving me you will be keeping *my* commandments." (indicating the progressive force of both verbs and the emphatic use of "my.") (My translation) *Third*, we will constantly study the written revelation (Bible) to better understand both Him, His Son, and our proper relations with both. *Fourth*, we will express our knowledge and obedience to His will in our relationships, actions, and even our thoughts.

CHAPTER 6

WHAT IS MAN?

I have taught college classes in human development for over forty years and am well acquainted with the theories of Eric Erickson, (Berger, p. 40) Donald Super (Harvard) and my teachers concerning self –definition. Not until I discussed this subject with a very consecrated group of my friends did I come to believe that the social sciences have a fundamentally flawed approach to the issue.

The social sciences approach the issue as something that the person must discover about himself if he/she is to have a successful life. Consider however, we don't ask something we make to discover its purpose. We design and build it for a purpose. Therefore, both as individuals *and* as a race it is only logical to ask the Creator what He intends as the purpose and nature of His creation, man. This constitutes an important part of the relationship between man and his Creator.

We reach an even deeper level of this understanding when the question becomes very personal and we ask "What is God's purpose for me at this point in time and with the background and resources He has given me?"

To develop a Christian self-definition one must look at what the

Scriptures say about man. After all, who can better define the creation than the Creator? As you will see events modify the definition.

The question of "What is Man?" seems to involve at least three areas: 1) his nature, 2) his purpose and duties and 3) his current state.

Man's Nature

Genesis recounts that God determined to "make man in our image, after our likeness" (Genesis 1:26) and that "God created man in His own image, in the image of God created He him, male and female created He them." (Genesis 1:26a, 27.) Theologians find specifying the characteristics of likeness to God much easier to define than the concept of "image of God." One writer, Spire (*Normative Spheres)* lists these as basic likenesses: personality, self-transcendence, intelligence, morality, gregariousness, and creativity.

In Genesis 2:7 the Scriptures say that "And Jehovah God formed man of dust of the ground and breathed into his nostrils the breath of life and man became a living soul." The word for soul according to Strong (Strong) is "*nephash*" which he defines as "a breathing creature." Brown, Driver and Briggs (Brown) in the first definition, define this word as "that which breathes, the breathing substance or being." He ties this to the Greek *psuchee*, of the Septuagint as "animal, the soul, the inner being of man."

The statement in Genesis 2:7 gives enough evidence to indicate that man's basic nature may be defined as a soul or spirit dwelling in a body made of the dust of the earth, but may also indicate that the two cannot be separated and the being still be a "man." If separated you have a ghost and a cadaver. Paul seems to support this view in 1 Corinthians 15:35—58.

His Purpose and Duties

God in Genesis 1:28 and again after the flood in Genesis 9:1 states the duties of man. These include: be fruitful and multiply, replenish the earth and subdue it, and have dominion over the fish...birds...every living thing. We can add to this the implied command in John 4:24, "God is a Spirit and they that worship Him must (*dei* - Moulton (Moulton) defines this verb as "it is binding, it is necessary, it behooveth, it is proper, it is necessary.) worship in spirit and truth." The context indicates that the place and time are not important. We might also add Ecclesiastes 12:13 "Fear God and keep His commandments, for this is the whole duty of man." More importantly Jesus in Matthew 22:37 — 40 (and elsewhere) states "Thou shalt love (*agapee* – not our English "love") the Lord thy God with all thy heart and with all thy soul and with all thy mind. This is the great and first commandment. And a second like unto it is this, Thou shalt love thy neighbor as (*hos* - Moulton (Moulton) define as, "as, like as.") thyself. On these two commandments the whole law hangeth, and the Prophets." The word translated love in this passage is *agape*. This love is a commitment and an unselfish desire to do what is best for the object. It is commanded, so it requires a decision to obey, not emotions, though these may follow.

The Ethical State of Man

Man in his first state was innocent and good. The sin recorded in Genesis 3:1—7 changed this. Man had the opportunity not only to be innocent but righteous because God placed a tree in the garden and instructed him that he must not eat of it. (Genesis 2:16, 17) This gave man the opportunity to decide to either obey or not to obey. If man made the decision to obey it brought him out of strict innocence into righteousness.

History tells us that man decided not to obey and became a sinner in rebellion against God. For the man the changes first included the ground was cursed "for thy sake." (Genesis 3:17—19) Whether this was a necessary condition to prevent rampant sin, or the result of Adam's action may be disputed. Second, he would eat only by toil. Third, the ground would tend to bring forth unpleasant things, not the eatable things he required. Romans 8:22, 23 indicates that the entire creation was affected. Finally, Genesis 3: 19 states that Adam was dust and he would return to dust. Obviously, it applies as well to women. On the other hand his duties remained much the same. The command to "Be fruitful and multiply" of Genesis 1:28 is repeated in Genesis 8:17 and 9:1.

Theologians have made much of the results of this sin including the unscriptural doctrine of total depravity. God still honored man after the fall, as expressed in Psalms 8:4—9 and Hebrews 2:6, 7. In the Psalm the writer states that God made man "but little lower than God, crownest him with glory and honor, Thou makest him to have dominion over the works of thy hand and has put all things under His feet;" Hebrews 2:7, quoting the LXX, makes it "a little lower than the angels."

On the other hand sin separated God and man. Romans 3:9—18, 23 states the status of man. All men sin, none is righteous...none fears God. Paul states in Romans 6:23 that the result of sin is death. Jesus states the result of sin in Matthew 7:13, 14. Sin leads to destruction.

The doctrine of total depravity says that man is "by nature" evil and cannot do anything good unless God works a miracle to change his nature. If this were true, then God the Creator is the author of evil. On the other hand it is better to translate the passages (e.g. Ephesians 2:3) "in the natural course of things." (Jesus by an "unnatural" or supernatural act changed this.) The passages which some use to teach that man can not of his own will respond to God (Romans 5:6, etc.) are best translated, as the ASV (The Bible, ASV) does, "weak," A translating "without power" should come from *adunaos,* the alpha negative prefixed to the word for power. The word used is *asthenos* which means, "weak, lacking enough strength." Man clearly could not of himself accomplish salvation, but the commands of Scripture (e.g. Acts 2:38, Acts 17:30) clearly places the determining action in the hands of man. It is certainly true (Romans. 3:9) that all men have sinned. Peter in 2 Peter 3:9 bluntly states God is "not wishing that any should perish, but that all should come to repentance." The verb "wishing" is *boulomenos (*Moulton, "to be willing, disposed, intend, to choose, to desire, appoint.) indicating not a simple wish, but a well laid plan. God planned it so that no one who would obey His plan would perish.

The associated doctrine that God predestined men to heaven or hell before creation is also false. The very passage used to support this doctrine (Romans 8:28-30) refutes it. This is one sentence and it begins with a limiting condition that controls the rest of the sentence. It is only about "those who love God" that he writes verses 28b through 30. The love here is the one commanded by Jesus (Matthew 22:37—39) and since it is command obeying it must be the result of a decision. You decide to be among those that love God and are therefore among those who were called, foreordained, justified and glorified.

The Change Jesus Accomplished for Christians

We must begin with the statement, cited above (2 Peter 3:9) that "God is... not wishing (made it his considered plan) that any should perish." This also states that He did not select only a limited number, as some teach. In the selection of those who will be saved God is completely impartial. (Romans 2:11) The factor that decides the issue is man's free obedience.

The book of Hebrews, especially chapter 8, recounts the miraculous change that Jesus accomplished for those who would accept him. Christ by the miracle of His atoning death changed the means for salvation from obedience to law to justification through faith (belief) and obedience to a few basic commands. Romans 3:21 tells us God's justification came apart from law. (*Dikiosunee* here as in other places is mistranslated righteousness and should be translated "justification".) (See Lard and Reese.) Paul writes that we are now free from the "curse" of the law. (Galatians 3:13) He then states that we are now children of God (Galatians 4:1—7) and His heirs. (Also see Romans 8:15—17)

Christians now have a new purpose. God created them (Ephesians 2:10) for good (The Greek word is *agathos* which means ethically good.) works. They have a new spirit (Ephesians 4:23, 24) in a renewed mind, "and that ye be renewed in the spirit of your mind, 24. And put on the new man, that after God hath been created in righteousness and holiness of truth." They no longer fear death. (1 Corinthians 15:56, 57)

Our Status as Christians

The things just said have important implications. We have freedom from "The Law" but have good works as our purpose and are subject to the "royal law" or "law of our King" (James 2:8) perhaps better stated in Jesus' summary of the two great commandments. (Matthew 22:37—40.) Paul in Romans Chapter 8 adds characteristics of our existence. We are under no condemnation. (Verse 1) We are not in "flesh" (a metaphor for secular living) but in spirit. (Verse 9) We don't walk after the flesh but after the spirit. (Verse 4) We are the adopted children of God. (Verses 14, 15) We are therefore His heirs. (Verse 17) Our sufferings are not to be compared with the glory to be revealed. (Verse 18) We await the redemption of the body. (Verse 23) God goes on helping our weakness even in prayer. (Verse 26) If we love him (a conscious, voluntary decision) then "He is working all *things* into ethically good *things*."(Verse 28) (My translation) Those who *chose* to love Him are foreordained to be conformed to the image of Christ. (Verse 29) They are called, justified, glorified. (Verse 30) No one can be against them effectively. God will give them all things. (Verses 31—3) No one can separate them from His love. (Verses 35, and 37—39.) No one can lay a charge against them. (Verse 33) They are more than conquerors. (Verse 37) God places great value on them. (Verse 32)

What should Christians think about their physical bodies? *First*, they can dishonor their bodies. (Romans 1:24) Paul details some things that dishonor them in Romans 1; 24—27. *Second*, Christ will give our mortal (dying) bodies life. (Romans 8:11) *Third*, our bodies are members of Christ and we must not join them to harlots. (1 Corinthians 6:15) *Fourth* our bodies are "temples (The Greek word is *naos*, a sanctuary, not *heron*, a building.) of (no article) holy spirit which is in you, which you have from the God...glorify God in your body." (1 Corinthians 6:19, 20) Paul teaches that in marriage authority (not power) over the body of each partner is given the other (1 Corinthians 7:4, 5) partner in the marriage. Finally, the scriptures clearly teach the resurrection of the body. (1 Corinthians 15:35-54)

How Then Should the Christian Define Himself as Man?

First, a Christian should define himself as a child of God, made in the image of God, and valuable enough to God for Him to send His Son to die for his redemption. Conversely he should conceive of himself as a sinner saved from eternal destruction only by the justification offered by unmerited mercy through Jesus' sacrifice. *Second*, he should see his function as good works particularly those related to his function as a holy priesthood. (1 Peter 2:9) As this priest he functions to bring men to God in subjection and worship. *Third, h*e will see himself as in a sense a battle field between a law of his mind and a law of sin that dwells in him (Romans 7:15 — 8:2) in which the mind, renewed by Christ, (Romans 12:2) will constantly work to subdue the sin within. In this he is assured that so long as his mind is committed to Christ he is not subject to condemnation. (Romans 8:1, 2)

How Will This Affect How He Deals With Life?

First, it should cause the Christian to present his body as a living sacrifice (Romans 12:1) in Christ's service. This means that the Christian will live to serve Christ. He will judge every activity by how it relates to his faithfulness to that commitment. The Christian will accept the roles God has assigned and fulfill the duties to which God calls him.

The Christian will seek to obey the teaching of Paul in Philippians Chapter 4 when he commands that we rejoice always (Verse 4), and that we be anxious in nothing. (Verse 6) He also directs that we are to manage both our mental life and behavior (Verses 8, 9) by God's teaching through the Apostles. This includes purity in thought with emphasis on the honorable, the just, the pure, the lovely, the things of good report, virtue and praise. In Verse 9 Paul writes "The things which ye both learned and received and heard and saw in me, these things do." (This is an imperative verb in the present (durative) tense and so this is a command for on-going action.)

It means that the Christian will always be prepared for spiritual battle. (Ephesians 6: 10, 11) He will also be prepared to love (agapee) without hypocrisy. He will seek to obey all of Paul's injunctions in Romans 12:9—21. As a list, this is something like what follows.

- He will abhor that which is evil; cleave to that which is good.
- He will be tenderly affectionate to other Christians, in honor prefer other Christians.
- He will be diligent not slothful.
- He will rejoice in hope.
- He will be patient in tribulation.
- He will be constant in prayer.
- He will communicate to the needs of the saints.
- He will be hospitable. (literally a friend to strangers)
- He will bless not curse those that persecute him.
- He will rejoice with those that rejoice, weep with those that weep.
- He will be of the same mind with Christians.
- He will concentrate on the lowly, not the high things.
- He will not be wise in own his own opinion.
- He will not render evil for evil.

- He will take thought of all things honorable in the sight of God.
- He will live at peace.
- He will not avenge himself.

Jesus (Matthew 5:10—12) commands (Verse 12) His followers to "rejoice and be glad" when they are persecuted because of their faith in Him. Much more could be written, but these will indicate the attitude that the Christian should have toward himself and his life.

How Should the Christian Approach Life Relationships

Of perhaps equal importance is his attitude *toward other men.* (Much of this is stated in the previous paragraph.) He will see in them the potential, yet the defects, he sees in himself. He will extend love (*agapee*) to all men.

In his *relationship with other Christians* he will extend that love as to fellow heirs and brothers in Christ. This love (*agapee*) must always be sincere (Romans 12:9). He will also be "having an affectionate family relationship in honor giving preference to one another." (Verse 10) (My translation attempts to recognize the two words for love that appear in the verse which are *not agapee.* The two words which Paul uses, p*hiladelphia* and *philostorgoi,* appear in combination. First, *pileee* appears as a combined word for "affection" with the word for "brother." Second, he combines the word for affection with the word for family love. "Giving preference" may indicate that the Christian gives preference to other Christians as contrasted to his relation to non-Christians. (Greek has another word which does not appear in the New Testament for sexual love.) Paul in 1 Corinthians 12:12—27 indicates the nature of the relationship between obedient Christians in such phrases as ""in one Spirit we were all baptized into one body...whether one member suffereth, all the members suffer with it; or one member is honored, all the members rejoice with it." The closeness of the intended relationship between Christians emphasized in this passage is often sadly lacking in the modern church.

Within the society he will be a law-abiding citizen. (Romans 13:1-7) *Within the church* he will accept the guidance of the leadership of the church (1 Peter 5:5, Hebrews 13:17, 1 Corinthians 16:16) as a voluntary action. (Obviously this does not apply to persons like Diotrephes.) (3 John 9—11) In another chapter we will deal with the relationships within the family.

CHAPTER 7

A BIBLICAL VIEW
OF THE CHURCH

*M*any sources in Biblical theology supply information concerning the nature of the church and its mission. Much of this is important, but for our purposes we want to seek to define how the Christian should see the church, and his/her relationship to it.

What the Church Is Not.

Too many in our day treat the church as if it were a place to make social contacts, a kind of low fee country club. With that, some consider it a place to be entertained. Buildings and programs are designed for this purpose, particularly when planners think of the youth of the church. It becomes a kind of baby-sitting service, a place it is good to send (take) the kids, a place where there are programs to keep each age group occupied. Many make their choice of congregations on the basis of what that congregation supplies.

Perhaps others take a more utilitarian approach. For some it is good business for the one engaged in business or a profession to be a member of a church. One of my employers attended the congregation I did because it was good business, and his brother attended the Methodist church for the same reason. In a bit of the reverse, but the same motivation, many consider it a good place to get a "hand-out." Some make touring various churches for charitable hand-outs a vocation.

A third group seeks a church that will give them the right kind of feelings. This may constitute an opportunity to contact "things spiritual." It may be a place where you can feel good, or get enthused, or find excitement. It may be a place where you get to hear a type of music that makes you feel in ways that you consider positive.

On the negative side, those who reject the church look at it as a place suitable only for the impractical and visionary thinker, with no place for the ones who are the real thinkers or leaders in the society.

All of these views have one dominating fault. *They are wrong!* The church is *not* a place. It is *not* a building. Our God does not dwell in a building made by hands. (This makes references to the church building as "God's house" inappropriate.) (Acts 17:24) It is not anything physical. In fact, it is made up of people, but a very *special kind* of people. The people who make up the church have been *born anew and born from above.* (John 3:3 – *anothen* can be translated "again" or "from above.") *Only God can add a person to the church,* (Acts 2:47) and He has set clear conditions for admission to the church in His word, particularly in Acts the only book in the world where a non-Christian asks an Apostle what he must do to be saved and receives a divinely inspired answer. .

What the Church Should Be for the Christian?

First it is a group to which the Christian gives his/her supreme political loyalty. It is as Peter says a *holy nation.* (1 Peter 2:9) The description as "holy" comes from the verb meaning "to cut, to separate, to divide" and as an adjective it means separated and set apart. This nation is composed of persons who are called of God (Romans 8:30, 9:24, 1 Corinthians 1:9, etc.) who also lead a holy and separated life. (Ephesians 4:1—3, Romans 1:7) We owe Christ, the King, absolute obedience. Romans 6: 22 told the Christians in Rome that they were those who," freed from sin and made slaves (*doulothentes)* to God were having their fruit into sanctification and in the end, eternal life." (My translation) Therefore, the church (not a denomination) merits our supreme political loyalty. It is the Kingdom of God.

Second, the church defines the Christian's ethnicity. He is part of the *people of God.* (1 Peter 2:9, 10) These people are the children of their Father, God, the King. (Romans 8:29) They are brothers to Jesus and to *every* other Christian. ("Brother" is frequently used referring to fellow Christians see 2 Corinthians 1:2; 2:13.)

Third, the church is the Christian's *truest* family. God as Father is head of the family, (2 Corinthians 6:18) "I will be to you a Father." We are his adopted children and so have the privilege of calling him "Abba." (I understand that this is an Aramaic word derived from baby talk meaning "daddy.") (Romans 8:15; Galatians 4:6, 7) This makes us heirs of God our Father. (Galatians 4:7) Jesus is pictured as the elder brother. (Romans 8:17, 29, Hebrews 2:10-18) Several elements of the idea appear here: many sons, called them brethren, children God gave, the liberating older brother and the understanding older brother.

As Christian we have God has given us a command to *agapate* the brotherhood. (1 Peter 2:17) *Agapee* is not adequately defined with the English word, "love." This word means "a conscious commitment to the best interest of the one loved." Christians decide to give this commitment, as an obedience to God. The distinguishing characteristic of the brotherhood is *agapee.* (John 13:34, 35) C. S. Lewis in *The Four Loves* (Lewis, 1987) gives an excellent discussion of the meanings of the four Greek words translated "love." He demonstrates that this *agapee* is the love which makes all the other "loves" good. I object to the spiritualizing of *agapee* by so many theologians. It is a word stating a command to be obeyed, so must be simply defined.

Though *agapee* should be had for all men, those within the brotherhood must have a deeper commitment for other members of the church, "especially toward them, that are of the household of faith." (Galatians 6:10) Romans 12:10 uses both p*hiladelphia* and *philostorgoi* to describe the love among Christians. (The verse reads, translated literally, "the affection for brothers into one another having the affections of a family, in the honor giving preference to one another.") (My translation) This combines the love of friends with family affection. Hebrews 13:1 makes *agapee* a command to be obeyed and uses the present-durative tense so it is to be a continuous obedience. ("Let" used in most translations means in English either a wish or permission. It is the word often used to translate the third person imperative which for which English has no parallel. Many times it is, as here, a command.) There should be a different feeling toward fellow Christians than that toward those outside the church. Christians are brothers and children of God. Others are not.

Fourth the church is metaphorically a body of which the Christ is the head. (Colossians 1:17, 18) The picture (metaphor) places Christ as the head and the church as all the rest of the body. The body in everything is subject to the head. (Christ) (Ephesians 5:23, 24, Ephesians 1:22, 23) He alone has final authority. (Matt. 28:17) He exercises this through the apostles and prophets. (Ephesians 2:19—22) This continues though it may have had a somewhat different meaning for those in the first century. In this passage we have reference to the total group of Christians as God's household. (There is no article with "spirit" in Verse 22 so it may be in the Holy Spirit, or in the spirit of the church.) The body is the instrument through which the intents of the head are accomplished. All nourishment, thought, decisions and breath comes through the head.

Fifth, the church is a priesthood which includes every Christian. Peter (1 Peter 2:5, 9) makes this clear when he describes the church as a holy priesthood, and a royal priesthood. The function of every Christian includes being a priest. First Peter 2:5 describes part of this work as offering up spiritual sacrifices. This necessitates service to others since sacrifices were mostly made in behalf of someone else.

What Should the Church Do For Me?

Acts 2:42 describes four basic services the Christian should expect from the church. *First,* the church should provide the teaching of the Apostles. Jesus sent His apostles (and us) to make students. (Matthew 28:19) The church must provide the avenue for us to accomplish this. *Second,* the church should provide each Christian a genuine fellowship. This includes help in need, but also companionship, advice, encouragement, sharing with others both physically and spiritually and the joy of the deepest and best friendship. Sometimes it will include comfort, sometimes exhortation and reproof. *Third,* the church should provide the Christian opportunities for the Lord's Supper. (The Breaking of *The* Bread) *Fourth,* the church will provide the Christian the support of a dynamic prayer life.

What I Should Do for the Church?

Being a part of this nation, family, priesthood implies that the Christian do things in order to be a part of the Church. *First,* he must submit his/her body as a living sacrifice in fulfilling Christ's purposes in the Church. (Romans 12:1) *Second.* he must function as a good citizen of the nation. He must make the Church his primary ethnicity. He must accept Christ as the head of the Church and (through the apostles) his/her source of knowledge, strength, spiritual nourishment, directions for coordinating work with other Christians, comfort and joy. *Third,* he must give the fullest fellowship, love, respect. assistance, comfort, extortion, and kinship to any fellow Christian. *Fourth,* he must serve as a priest bringing others to God. *Fifth,* he must diligently study God's revelation. (2 Timothy 2:15) *Sixth,* he must make it his/her ambition and full commitment to be a good teacher. (Hebrews 5:12) *Seventh,* he must be prepared to suffer persecution as a good soldier. *Finally,* he must, without hypocrisy, have *agapee* for every other Christian as a family member (Romans 12:9) and every other person as a neighbor.

Just a Final Thought

I have not mentioned some things because they are expressions of what we have mentioned. Stewardship is part of the exercise of fellowship. Attending the meetings of Christians is also a part of this fellowship. These meetings are in many places, for many purposes, and *never* a way of serving God. They are a way we serve each other. The pagan gods required these "services" to keep them happy. Our God needs nothing from our hands. (Acts 17:25) We "go to church [the assembly]" to receive the four items (Acts 2:42) that *we* need to grow into the "measure of the stature of the fullness of Christ." (Ephesians 4:13)

CHAPTER 8

THE CHRISTIAN WORLD VIEW AND THE FAMILY

*H*ow should a Christian regard the home? Since the home comprehends several parts and roles, this question raises a variety of questions related to the home. These include a number of ethical issues.

Sin And the Home

The Scriptures teach that marriage must not be dishonored. (Hebrews 13:4.) This can happen when an individual commits certain sins. These include fornication (This a word that is becoming antique and is not used in many translations. It is defined as sexual intercourse involving unmarried people.), adultery, homosexuality, and divorce. First Corinthians 6:15—20, Galatians 5:19—21, Ephesians 5:3, Colossians 3:5, Hebrews 13:4 condemn fornication and adultery. Romans 1:26—28 teaches that homosexuality is degrading and a sin giving evidence that those who practice it are no longer acceptable to God. First Corinthians 6:15—19 clearly forbids any promiscuous sex.

The Scriptures teach a high respect for marriage. Hebrews 13:4 says literally "Honored the marriage in all (masculine), the marriage bed (by metonymy sexual intercourse) unsoiled (by metanomy undefiled, pure), fornicators and adulterers God will judge." (condemn) (My translation) When the English translators use "let" they usually have encountered a third person imperative. We have no third person imperative in English, so the" let" often seems permissive, when it is actually a command. In this case there is no verb except "judge". I believe, with the translators, that the imperative of "is" is implied by context and so it should be understood as a command that marriage be honored and intercourse unsoiled. It is interesting to note the gender of "all" is masculine, as well as the words for adulterers and fornicators, perhaps indicating that this may be more an issue for males, since women have so much to gain from marriage. On the other hand our culture has made both sins common for both sexes. It may be that "all" here refers to the generic of man (*anthropos*) which is masculine and includes all people. The statement that God will judge (condemn) fornicators prohibits premarital sex (occasional or habitual such as living together without marriage) with a very stern warning. The Bible also gives us an example that marriage is honored when those who come to marriage are virgin in the accounts of the birth of God's only-begotten Son. (Matthew 1, Luke 1)

For our day the impact of these prohibitions may be horrific. Anyone who has not repented for these actions is still guilty of them. If the person is still guilty of them he has no hope of eternal life. (1 Corinthians 6:9, 10) Verse eleven gives the assurance of forgiveness if the person repents.

A Possible Command to Marry

The only implied approval of celibacy appears in Revelation 14:4 where it speaks of men as pure because they had not defiled themselves with women but were virgins. . The book of Revelation is highly symbolic so the teaching is not clear. Paul's statement in 1 Timothy 4:2, 3 is quite clear where he says that "through the hypocrisy of men that speak lies, branded in their conscience with a hot iron; 3) forbidding to marry, and commanding to abstain from meats God created to be received with thanksgiving by them that believe and know the truth." Paul clearly condemns as false teachers those who forbid marriage.

Jesus on the other hand in Matthew 19:10—12 commands in verse

12 that all but the three groups which He has listed as exceptions should "receive it" (the marriage uniting a man and a woman into one flesh). The word "receive" is a third person singular present active imperative. We have no third person imperative so the translators have translated it with "let" which seems permissive not imperative. Literally it says "I am ordering the persons who have the power to be receiving (Moulton defines it as "make room for, precede, progress, yield accord, admit to approbation and esteem, regard cordially.") it." (My translation) The only available antecedent for "it" is Verse 5 which says, "For this cause shall a man leave his father and mother and shall cleave to his wife; and they shall become one flesh." Jesus has just listed the exceptions, those incapable of reproduction, and those whose service for the Kingdom make it inadvisable.

The issue becomes more complex when you read 1 Corinthians 7:2—4. In Verse 2 Paul commands men and women to be having wives and husbands. (Again the translators make this seem as permission by using "let." It is a third person imperative in each case, so Paul is giving an order. "I command that each man or woman be having his own wife and each woman be having her own husband." (My translation indicating the imperative verbs) This agrees with the command that Jesus gave in Matthew 19:12.

Paul seems to contradict himself in 1 Corinthians 7:8 and 26 and 27. In Verse eight he advises against marriage. In Verse 26 and particularly in Verse 27 he seems to reinforce the advice. The reader must take these verses in context. In Verses six and seven he writes "and this I am saying according to a concession, not according to a commandment, and I am wishing all men (mankind) to as (like) also myself. " (My translation) The reader must decide whether this refers to the preceding five verses, or to the rest of the chapter. In Verse twelve he again denies divine authority for what he is writing. He again denies that he has divine authority in Verse twenty-five when he writes "I have no commandment of the Lord, but I give my judgment." In 1 Corinthians 7:40 Paul seems to reassume some of the authority of divine revelation when he writes "and I think that I also have the Spirit of God." This last half of the verse may be literally translated "And I am thinking I also to be having a divine spirit." (My translation) There are no articles with the words "spirit" or "god." Without the article, *theos* is usually considered a reference to deity; with the article it refers to the one living God. He explains his advice in verse 26 when he says "by reason of the distress that is upon us."

Is Paul trying to confuse us? I doubt it. He recognizes the command in Verse 2, but believes that conditions at that time made it wise to *postpone* obedience to the command. He is very clear that marriage is not a sin. In Verse 28 he states it bluntly. In Verse 36, I understand that he is speaking to the father of the woman, who, in that day, had the duty of providing her with a husband. Delaying this action seems best to him, but in verse 40 he says it is his judgment. The understanding of these references to marriage involves deciding whether, in Verse 6, Paul is referring to what proceeds of what comes after Verse 6.

To summarize this section we would first not accuse Paul of being confusing in his teaching. It seems that under ordinary circumstances both he and Jesus give commands to those capable of marriage that they be married. He allows for a delay in the action until the circumstances are favorable.

Finally and very importantly we must understand this within the culture in which it was written. Romantic love as a basis for marriage is less that 400 years old even in western society. Before that time, as well as even today in the Far East, marriage is a contract between families, and it is a sacred duty of the father to arrange marriages for his children. The "track record" of their marriages is reported as 95% happy. In our romantic love system marriage is experienced as between 5% and 10% happy. More than half of our marriages end in divorce. If you considered as marriage our "unmarried living with each other" which seems to be becoming the norm, it would be even a lower proportion of happy marriages.

Teaching Regarding Divorce

Matthew 19:3—9 and Mark 10:2—12 teach that God limits divorce to occasions of adultery and intends marriage to be as long as both shall live. In my opinion Paul gives an additional reason for acceptable divorce when an unbelieving spouse refuses to live with the Christian. (1 Corinthians 7:12-15) This can only be if the *unbeliever* refuses to continue the marriage. However, in verse 15 Paul in "let him depart" commands (an imperative) that action, and uses the perfect participle to say "the brother or sister is not under continuing bondage." (My translation) I believe this leaves the believer free to marry again, but only to a Christian. (2 Corinthians 6:14-16) Don't fail to remember that in this case the unbelieving partner who leaves has no hope of eternal life unless he becomes a Christian.

Teaching As To Separation

First Corinthians 7:10, 11 teaches that a woman is not to "separate" (uses the word for sever, sunder, disunite, not the usual word for divorce) from her husband. She must not let anything separate her from her husband (job, relatives, even children); if she does she should remain unmarried or be reconciled. The alternative given is reconciliation, and it is implied that this separation is only permitted when reconciliation is considered the normal future action. This gives an option to the woman who suffers abuse from her husband. This abuse may be physical or it may be psychological.

It is interesting to note that God may enforce alimony and child support. The woman in that day had very few ways to exist outside of marriage except family support or prostitution. Paul in 1 Corinthians 7:11 does not have a direct command to the husband, but has two imperative verbs as to the wife. ("but if she depart I order that she remain unmarried or I order that she be reunited to her husband.") (My translation showing the two third person imperative verbs.). The last phrase in the verse may be translated literally "and a husband not to be neglecting a wife". The context implies a command to the husband. The word for "neglecting" is not that for divorce but is "send away, dismiss, care not for, forsake, leave remaining or alone." (Thayer) Paul seems to indicate by an implied imperative form of "is, to be" that the husband in a separation must still provide for his wife.

Marriage and Family Are Second to Devotion to God.

In Luke 14:26 and Matthew 10:35, 37 Jesus indicates that devotion to God takes precedence over marriage and family. In most circumstances the devotion to God strengthens the institution of marriage. Jesus states that having greater affection (Greek *phileo)* for family members than for Him (emphatic) means the person is not worthy of Christ. Luke makes it a requirement that the person "hate" his father, mother, wife, children brothers and sisters even his own life or he does not "have the power" (My literal translation) to be His disciple. Although the word translated "hate" here carries the meaning "hate, detest, pursue with hatred" (Thayer) Many translators, (and some lexicons) considering the difference in cultures, think in western thought it may be translated "love less, slight, overlook." This seems to follow the contrasts John makes in his first epistle between love (*agapee*) and hate (*miseo*). Note, however, that this requires that in the love of *agapee* (commitment, putting the interest of the other first) for God takes precedence over devotion to family or any of its members.

Qualifications for Christian Marriage

Christian marriage may only occur when both persons are Christians. This is clearly stated in 2 Corinthians 6:14—18. It can only be a Christian marriage when (1 Corinthians 7:39) it is "only in *the* Lord." It is further qualified by Jesus comments in Matthew 19:11, 12 when He states those who are exempt from marriage. The exemptions are for those who cannot reproduce themselves and those who because of service to the Kingdom of God find marriage is inadvisable.

Special Functions of the Home.

God has assigned at least four special functions to the home. *First,* one of the most obvious functions is that it is to be the location of sexual and reproductive activity. We discussed this in the section concerning sin and the home. Paul further reinforces this teaching in 1 Corinthians 7:3—5. In verse 3 the translators have again used "let" which seems permissive because of the fact that English does not have a third person imperative. The verb is third person imperative and has the meaning "I am ordering the husband to be giving to the wife what is owed, and likewise the wife to the husband." (My translation) The Greek word for "what is owed is *opheilan.* (Moulton defines this as "a debt, by metonymy a duty or what is due.) Based on the context this seems to be a reference to sexual activity. Verse 5 seems to indicate that neither is to refuse sexual relations except for brief periods devoted to prayer and this must be with the consent of both parties.

The *second* function given to the home is caring for those family members in need. Jesus reinforced this in Mark 7:10—13. Jesus clearly indicates that honoring parents includes specifically giving them support in their need or old age. Paul further reinforces this in 1 Timothy 5:4 and 16. This speaks of widows, but certainly includes any indigent parent. Paul adds (verse 8) that anyone not providing for the need of his own household is worse than a pagan. Only when there are no relatives available does this become the duty of the church. (Verse 16)

The *third* and possibly the most important function of the home is teaching. This includes teaching the spouse. In 1 Corinthians 14:35 the verb "ask" is another third person imperative and so Paul is ordering the women to ask their husbands at home. It is also a present tense which indicates ongoing (durative) practice and so it is a continuing process. The wife also has a responsibility to teach her husband (1 Peter 3:1) but it is to be by behavior not words particularly if he is pagan. In Titus 2:3 the older women are to be teachers of the *kalos* (the good, useful, beautiful, virtuous). Verse 4 applies this "teachers of the good" when it tells the older women "in order that they may go on making wise the young women (to be – implied) affectionate to husbands and affectionate to children." (My translation) Children constitute the final group that must be taught. Paul places this responsibility on the father in Colossians 3:20, 21 and Ephesians 6:1—4. In Ephesians 6:4 Paul commands the fathers to "bring them up (imperative verb, present tense, so a command for continuing action)" his children, "in *paideia* ("education, training, nurture, instruction, discipline, correction, chastisement" - Moulton) and *nouthesia* ("warning, admonition" Moulton) of *the* Lord. " This parallels the commands to the Jews in Deuteronomy 6:4—9. (This is the great "*Shema*" passage.) That passage even outlines the program of teaching for the home. It commands teaching 1) when you lie down – evening, 2) when you rise up – morning 3) when you sit in your house – times of relaxation 4) when you take a trip. It adds that God teaching must clearly be 1) the basis of actions in the home (hand), 2) the basis of judgments (eyes), 3) the standard for decisions in the house (on the door posts) and 8) the standard for decisions in the courts (gates where courts were held). Remember that in Ephesians 6:4 fathers are ordered (an imperative verb) not to provoke the children to wrath, and in Colossians 3:21 they are ordered (an imperative verb) not to provoke their children. The Greek words make the command in Ephesians more sweeping, but they come from the same root meaning "to provoke, to irritate, exasperate, incite, stimulate," (Moulton) The reason for the command is "that they (the children) not be discouraged."

A *fourth* function of the home is hospitality. First Timothy 3:2 and Titus 1:8 make it an important qualification for leaders in the church. First Timothy 5:10 makes it a qualification for admission to the care of the church. Christians in general are commanded to exercise hospitality by 1 Peter 4:9 and Romans 12:13. Taken literally we can understand that this properly involves friendship to strangers. The Greek word is a combination of the word for friendship or affection, and the word "stranger." Is it a commentary on modern failure in this area that we no longer build a "guest" room in our houses? The first century home often had a *kataluma.* It was in this room that there was no place (*topos* – "place, locality" (Moulton)) for Mary and Joseph and in this room that the disciples prepared the Passover before Jesus was crucified.

The Relation Between Home and Church

The home is closely related to the church. For three centuries the church met in homes.(1 Corinthians 16:19, Romans 16:5, Acts 5:42; 12:12; 16:40; 20:8, 20) In the New Testament Paul uses the home as a figure of the church. (1 Timothy 3:14, 1 Corinthians 4:14-17) The home seems to be structurally related to Christ through the church. The chart that follows indicates the "line of command" in God's world. The family is one of the very important units in that line of command.

God's Line of Command (Leadership)

I

God alone has original (not derived) authority.

I

Jesus received all authority in heaven and on earth. (Matthew 28:18)

I

Jesus gave authority to the Apostles
to bind or loose *only* what had been bound and loosed in heaven.
(Matthew 16:19, *and* 18:18)

I

The Apostles and their associates wrote these things into Scripture.
These are now the voice of the Apostles for us.

I

Evangelists were sent to "set in order the things that are wanting" and "appoint" elders in every city." (This includes selection and teaching them what was needed.) (Titus 1:5)

I

The Elders (also called shepherd/teachers and supervisors) were appointed to supervise, teach, and care for the church. (Acts 20:28)

I   I

Servants (deacons) were to perform   I
tasks assigned by the   I
elders. (Acts 6:3—6)

I

Fathers are to rule well
their own house having
the children in subjection.
(1 Timothy 3:4, 5)

I   I

Wives were to be in subjection   I
to their own husbands.
(Ephesians 5:22. Colossians 3:18)   I

I   I

Children are to obey their parents. (Ephesians 6:1, Colossians 3:20)

Note: The *burden* of authority, leadership, guidance and teaching flows downward: the *privilege* of receiving those services flows upward. Children have more people seeking to serve, protect and teach them, but are free from the burden of leadership.

The Role of the Husband – Father

Relating to His Wife

The Scriptures *command* that the husband must have *"agapee"* for his wife. (Ephesians 5:25, Colossians 3:19) The English word love does not adequately express this idea. He must decide to commit himself to do in everything that which he sincerely believes is in the best interest of his wife regardless of the cost to himself. This includes following in the steps of Jesus which Peter teaches (1 Peter 2:21, 3:7—9) include dwelling with her in a knowledgeable way, giving honor to her, being of one mind with her, having compassion, giving pity as needed, being courteous, not giving evil for evil, but rather giving blessing. Paul in Colossians (above) forbids the husband being bitter toward his wife and commands that they become one. The expression in Ephesians 5:31, and in Genesis 2:24 (LXX) *is"kai esontai oi duo eis sarka mian.* "(And the two will be into one flesh.) The Hebrew was translated into Greek in the LXX by seventy of the best scholars of Jesus' day. The use of *eis* (into) may indicate a gradual process. Jesus uses the same expression in Matthew 19:6 and Mark 10:8. Even if there is a separation Paul commands (1 Corinthians 7:11) that the husband must not neglect (omit, send away) his wife. The passages from Ephesians and Colossians also indicate that the husband must offer his wife the services of a leader. (The word translated "be in subjection to" is *hupotasso* a term for the military relationship between the soldier and his superior, not that of master and slave.) The soldier accepts his superior's leadership in loyalty to his country. The wife accepts her husband's leadership in loyalty to her risen Lord. Incidentally, a good solder with a good superior will always tell the leader what he/she believes to be true even if it may not please the superior. Finally, 1 Corinthians 7:4 directs that the husband must grant is wife authority over his body, and accept authority over hers and in this not defraud her. (1 Corinthians 7:4, 5)

Relating to His Children

The most basic relationship the father has to his children is their teacher. This follows the pattern given in the "Shema" (Deuteronomy 6:4 – 9 where it begins with "Hear, O Israel:" The "Israel" that had just been numbered was the men of fighting age, and therefore those most likely to have families. There He gives the commands, even the program for teaching. (This is outlined above.) The New Testament follows this pattern when Ephesians 6:4 directs that the father bring the children up in the *paidea* of the Lord. This word has a disciplinary flavor. It was used of scourging criminals. He was also directed by the same verse to bring the children up in the *nouthesia* of the Lord. This word implies teaching and correction with words. The same verse forbids him to provoke to anger, irritate, or exasperate his children. Colossians 3:21 adds that the father must not to *erithudzete* (provoke, irritate, exasperate) them so that they will not be discouraged.

Relating to Gaining Christian Maturity

As a maturing Christian, we understand from Hebrews 5:12 that the husband should have the purpose of becoming a teacher. I read James 3:1 as not commanding people not to be teachers (since that would contradict the command in Hebrews) but asking if they are not becoming teachers because of the added responsibility. The syntax makes it very possible that this is a question, "Are many of you not becoming teachers...?" rather than a command not to become teachers. (The spelling of the verb *ginesthe* (become) as a command is precisely the same as the spelling in the indicative mode.) Translators have rendered it as a command because of the *mee* which usually does not occur in the indicative. Machen (1928, p. 197 section 478) writes "Questions expecting a negative answer are expressed by *mee* with the indicative." This translation does not contradict the implied requirement in Hebrews.

In the leadership of the church Paul (Ephesians 4:11) listed two permanent groups of workers: the evangelists and the shepherd/teachers. (The terms elders and bishops are indicated as referring to the last group in other passages.) Since Hebrews (5:12) indicates that the mature Christian man should be a teacher. Each husband should have as one of his objectives growing into being a good teacher. A description of what that man should be appears in both 1 Timothy 3 and Titus 1.

The Role of the Wife/Mother

As Respects Her Husband

Though some of the directions are not very popular today, the fact that the Scriptures teach them cannot be altered. Paul in Ephesians 5:22—33 teaches that the wife must subject herself (middle voice) to her husband in all things. The word used for subject is a military one indicating the loyalty of a soldier to his commanding officer, *not* the obedience of a slave. The middle voice makes accepting his leadership the wife's decision in obedience to God. The last verse (Verse 33) adds that she must respect (fear) her husband as a good soldier does his commanding officer. First Peter 3:1—5 adds that if her husband is an unbeliever, she it to use example not words to win him. First Corinthians 7:4 teaches that she must grant her husband authority over her body, accept it over his and not defraud him in this. (Verse 5) The Greek word is *exousia* from which we get "executive" not *dunamis* from which we get "dynamite." Translating the word "power" is a poor translation just as it is in John 1:12. Both are present tense so are a continuing pattern of live, not a once given obedience. First Peter 3:8, 9 directs that both she and her husband must be of the same mind, have sympathy, affection and humility, never returning evil for evil, but blessing.

As Respects Her Family

We have no commands to the mother as concerns her children. We assume that she will be a helper "meet for" (The LXX uses first *kata*, (according to) then *homoios* (like as) in Genesis 2:18 and 20.) an expression usually assumed to mean "suited to, adapted to, answering to" her husband in caring for (teaching) their children. (Genesis 2:20) We have two commands to wives in 1Timothy 5:8 and 14. The first directs both husband and wife that they must care for their own (men or women) or they are worse than infidels. The second teaches that younger women should get married and bear children. Titus 2 instructs older women that they must teach younger women to be lovers of children and lovers of husbands. The word for love here indicates intense affection.

As Respects Personal Public and Private Deportment

Titus 2:3—5 instructs the women be reverent in behavior, not slanderers (gossips), not alcoholics, and teachers of what is good. (This "good" is the word combining *kalos* and *didaskalos* meaning teaching things that are good, useful, productive of good things, as well as ethically good.) This last element is clearly a command. These verses also teach that women are to be self controlled, pure, workers at home, kind and submissive to their husbands.

Directions for their public deportment includes in particular three passages that have been difficult for many to manage. Many would like to understand the meaning of these as restricted to the culture of that day, but this view cannot be sustained since Paul based his commands to women on God's design in creation. (1 Timothy 2:13—15)

In 1 Timothy 2:9—12 Paul (inspired by the Holy Spirit) instructs women that they must adorn themselves in modest apparel without costly ornamentation but with good works. He also says that they were not to teach or exercise authority over a man. (*aneir)* (In Greek husband and man are the same word. Could this mean her husband?) He then instructs the women to remain quiet.

First Corinthians 11:1—16 commands that the woman must cover her head. This seems to apply to the public assemblies. This may well be conforming to local standards of decency or avoiding indication of an immoral character. This seems to be indicated in Verse 16. On the other hand Verse nine speaks of it as "having an authority on her head because of angels." This may be from the fact that the word we translate as angel (a transliteration) is also the one for messengers. It may be that commands this in order to clearly identify a married woman to strangers. (Have you heard of preachers who take off their wedding ring when they go away from home?)

First Corinthians 14:34, 35 forbids the woman to speak in the assemblies. (church) (The Greek word (*lalein*) used in both verses indicates casual speech not considered statements. Could it be a prohibition of chattering in the assembly?) There is another Greek word (*legein*) for considered discourse. Verse thirty-five directs that if a woman has a question she should ask her husband at home. The translation "let" found in most English translations is an unfortunate result of an effort to translate a third person imperative which English does not have as a grammatical form. In both Verses 34 and 35 the verb translated "let" is a present imperative verb meaning that Paul (inspired by The Holy Spirit) is commanding the women to "go on being silent in the church" (assembly) and to "go on asking their husbands at home." (My translation)

This does not relieve women of the responsibility for teaching. The example of Priscilla, who with her husband Aquila taught Apollos seems approved. (Acts 18:25, 26) Note that in this instance Priscilla is mentioned first. This often indicated that that person was the leader. You will note that they teach Apollos outside the assembly. Titus 2:3 and 4 makes the older women teachers of the good, particularly teachers of younger women. This may have been in homes, but it was still a duty with public implications. This passage has no verb. The writers often assumed the reader would insert a form of "to be" and did not write it. In the case the verb seems to be an imperative (command) form of "be."

The Role of the Child

The Duties of the Child

Ephesians 6:1—4 and Colossians 3:20, 21 defines the parent-child relationship. This directs children that they must obey their parents. Jesus taught this by His example. (Luke 2:51, 52) They also must honor their parents. On the other hand fathers must not provoke (exasperate) them. This should apply to both parents, and indicates a relationship of committed love and affection.

This honoring of parents has a practical side. "Honor" in the Greek comes from the word *timao* which has its root meaning in fixing value, appraising, and taxes. (Bromley) The Scriptures consistently teach the responsibility of support of parents in their old age. (Consider Exodus 20:12 and Deuteronomy 5:16.) Jesus enforces this in Mark 7:10—13 in His condemnation of the Pharisees. Paul firmly states this in 1Timothy 5:4, 8. In these verses Paul makes it a test of the sincerity of their Christian faith.

The Value of a Child

The scriptures consider barrenness to be a tragedy (Luke 1:7, 25) and child to be a blessing. (Luke 1:25, 31, 42) I believe that barrenness is a choice in most cases since adoption is possible. (I don't minimize the problems involved in adoption. My wife and I adopted two children, and have two birth children. If we had known the problems the adoptions would cause, we probably would have been too fearful to proceed. Modern psychological research has demonstrated that adopted children have a lifestyle more like their birth parents than their adoptive ones even if adopted at birth. We believe, however, that God worked blessings for us and for them by the relationship.) The scriptures teach that children are born (adopted) for a purpose. (Luke 1:14—17) Jesus blessed children and was angry when His disciples interfered with their coming to Him. (Matthew 19:13—15; Mark 10:13—16; Luke 18:15—17) The church included them in church groups. (Acts 21:5) With Christian parents they are holy. (1 Corinthians 7:14)

Grandparents

Duties of Grandparents

Older people (probably grandparents) have functions. Titus 2 seems to speak to these roles. It directs the grandfathers to be "temperate, grave, sober minded, sound in faith, in love, in patience." It directs grandmothers to be "reverent in demeanor, not slanderers (gossips) not enslaved to much wine, teachers of that which is good," This was in order that they might train the young women. Perhaps one of the strongest motivations for Godly behavior among older male Christians should be the fact that word for older men has the same root as that we translate "elder."

Duties of Younger Christians to Parents and Grandparents

The scriptures consistently teach that these older people must be honored, contrary to our modern society which worships youth. Leviticus 19:32 commands "Thou shalt rise up before the hoary head, and honor the face of the old man, and thou shalt fear thy God: I am Jehovah." The seriousness and emphatic nature of the command is emphasized by the two phrases which succeed and enforce it, "thou shalt fear thy God: I am Jehovah." The first commandment in the Decalogue concerning relations to other humans (Exodus 20:12) commands that every Israelite honor his/her mother and father. Paul's instruction (1 Timothy 5:1, 3, 4, 8) and the teaching of Jesus (Mark 7:8—13; Matthew 19:19) all emphasize the importance of this divine command.

Family Roles As Respects Salvation

Many cite Galatians 3:26—29 as stating there is no difference between the genders. Usually the statement about neither male nor female is taken out of context. The immediate context of the passage (v.28) says "There can be neither Jew nor Greek, there can be neither slave nor free man, there can be no male and female; for ye are all one (*man*) in Christ Jesus." Does this mean that now all people were descendents of Jacob or that none of the people were descendents of Jacob? That is a strange genealogy. Does it mean that all slaves were now free or all Christians were now slaves? The words here are not the ones for husband and wife. Does it mean that everyone would be able to bear children or that no one could? The simples and best answer is that God shows no favoritism as concerns salvation (forcibly stated in Romans 2:11) but the passage has nothing to do with earthly roles. These roles remain.

All of the teaching is part, however, of the total obedience that God requires of His people. First John 5:2, 3 clearly make this obedience necessary to obeying the most important of all commandments, that we love God with all that is in us. Jesus says in John 14:15 "if you are loving me, you will be keeping my commandments." (My translation indicating the durative nature of the verbs.)

Summary of the Christian View of the Home

- The home is sacred and must be held in high honor.
- Children are one of God's choice blessings.
- Given the opportunity, a Christian will be married, but only to another Christian and only "in the Lord."
- Leadership in the home is the burden God has laid on the husband/father.
- *Agapee* love is essential to the home as it is to the Christian life.
- Children must learn to obey their parents as minors, honor them all their lives, and support them if necessary in old age or illness.

CHAPTER 9

HOW SHOULD THE CHRISTIAN REGARD GENDER?

*T*his issue challenges the church in the area of maintaining Biblical authority. Every conservative group feels pressure concerning gender roles. An example of this occurred when professors from one college went to a conference related to the Restoration Movement (This is the reformation in the nineteenth century in which Alexander Campbell was an outstanding leader.) at another "conservative" graduate school. A graduate seminary student presented a paper on the subject. The leaders sponsoring the conference refused to allow the professors from this college an opportunity to see the text before it was given or to raise any questions in what was termed a "discussion" afterward. Most people consider both colleges within the Restoration Movement. If this represents the new point of attack on Biblical authority it represents a very crucial issue.

In America the communications media have mounted a major campaign to eliminate traditional views of gender. They constantly push the notion that there is no genuine difference between male and female roles casting women in roles both in employment, home and sports that seek to eliminate any gender difference. This extends to the concerted attempt to teach that homosexuality is acceptable if not desirable as a gender role. If it were not for the desire to make the person sexually seductive, they would seek to eliminate gender differences in clothing. This has come to the point that school authorities have difficulty in maintaining gender difference in bathroom and shower room facilities. In many ways this effort seeks to eliminate any specifically masculine role, and sometimes any feminine role, seeking for a kind of "unisex" world. In many areas it seeks to eliminate maternal, gentle, self-giving or submissive behavior.

Neither *Webster's Collegiate Dictionary* (Webster's) nor *Webster's Unabridged Dictionary* (Compton) gives a clear definition of "gender" as it functions in life. They give grammatical discussions, but Webster's *Collegiate Dictionary* gives the closest definition of it in life in general as "coloq, sex, male and female." C. S. Lewis does a much better job in his book of fiction, *That Hideous Strength.* (Lewis) He correctly implies that gender includes not only biological characteristics but roles for the individuals. English and especially Greek use gender when the element considered has no sex. (In English a ship may be feminine; in Greek there are many items for which gender is specified that have no sex.) He correctly defines gender as a role; and sex as one available feature of that role. God brought gender into existence in Genesis 1:27; 2:18—25. This passage has *no* mention of sex or reproduction. Roles are, however, assigned (Genesis 2:18, 20). Biblically, gender is a God given role. He who fails to function in that God given role finds himself in conflict with his Creator. This role (gender) includes physical characteristics, but also includes patterns of conduct, values, ways of self expression, assigned functions and possibly other factors.

The Bible Speaks of Two Genders

Early and later we are told that God made man male and female. (Genesis 1:27; 5: 2; Matthew 19:4; Mark 10:6). This also applies to the other living things in His creation, both animals and some plants (Those plants that do not have gender still have parts with gender.) It appears that a part of His design for the world includes the existence of two genders among most living things. God made some distinctions between the two genders and requirements of each gender in His law and in His dealing with people throughout Biblical history, and continues His instructions to the present through His inspired revelation.

Old Testament Directions Related to Gender

God created woman only after creating the male and finding no companion suited to him among the animals. (Genesis 2:18, 20—23) He states the purpose for the creation of the woman in Genesis 2:18, when He says "I will make him a help meet for him." ("Meet for" is an obsolete expression, but means "suited or adapted to." The LXX uses *kata auton* which is translated "according to him.") In general the Old Testament regulations worked to protect the woman.

The Old Testament almost always restricts battle service, leadership and the priestly function to men. The initial census counted only the men of fighting age. (Numbers 1:2, 3) Only men could be priests. (Numbers 3:15) Circumcision, the sign of the covenant, applied only to males. (Genesis 17:10-14) All of the respected national leaders were male except Deborah. (Judges 4) She tried to get Barak to take the leadership but he refused and it worked out to his discredit.

The Ten Commandments always required giving honor to both father and mother. (Exodus 20:12, Deuteronomy 5:16) The   Old Testaments contains many references and distinctions based on gender. It is clear that God intended the genders to have their distinctive roles, considered it an important distinction and was not pleased when men disregarded those distinctions. The sacrificial system often specified the sex of the sacrifice. Since this was usually male, it protected the female and provided for productivity.

The woman in Hebrew society had a respected place. In Numbers 27 the daughters of Zelophehad asked for inheritance rights through their deceased father who had no sons. Numbers 7:6, 7 says, "And Jehovah spake unto Moses saying, The daughters of Zelophehad speak right." God's will then granted them (and women in a similar situation) rights of inheritance, something which women in England had only in a restricted way until the late years of the 19th. century. Abraham loved Ishmael and did not want to sent him away, but he yielded to Sarah. The Leverite law protected women as widows. The Law also protected the woman taken captive and chosen as a wife, forbidding that she become a slave. (Deuteronomy 21:14) The giving of a writ of divorcement (which Jesus rejected) was a protection for the wife who was rejected. She could not be left in matrimonial limbo. These are only a few of a number of laws designed to protect the woman.

God opposes confusion of gender or attempts at gender reversal. God even condemns the wearing of the garments of the opposite sex as an abomination. (Deuteronomy 22:5)

New Testament Teaching and Gender

In the New Testament the distinction, male or female, does not exist as to salvation. (Galatians 3:28) Some have attempted to teach that this means there is no difference in their acceptable roles. If this were true, then all men would be slaves or all men free, all have the ability to produce children, or all not have the ability to produce children, all men would be Jews or all men would be Greeks.

The Scripture (Romans 1:26. 27) condemns reversal of gender roles and/or homosexual practices. (Compare also I Corinthians 6:9 for the last two groups condemned.) He repeats this teaching in 1Timothy 1:10. Paul teaches that men and women are given different (but complementary) roles in the Church. (1 Timothy 2:8—15, 1 Corinthians 7:2—5, 11:3—16) Additional details of this are given in Titus 1 and 2.

Gender is important in the New Testament. The term for "God" is always masculine. Jesus came as a male. Except for the prophetesses, the terms used for all the leaders in the church are masculine. Apostle, prophet, evangelist, elder, *episkopos*,(translated as bishop, the corruption of the word) shepherd, teacher, *diakonos* (twice translated Deacon, most often translated "minister" and is applied to the Apostles and other leaders) are all masculine nouns. The qualifications for church leadership (1 Timothy 3 and Titus 1) imply male leadership. The Scriptures describe the relation between Christ and His church in terms of gender. The church is called the bride of Christ by John indirectly in John 3:28, 29, directly in Revelation 21:2, 9. Jesus calls himself the bridegroom. (Matthew 9:15; Mark 2:19, 20; Luke 5:34, 35) On the other hand, the church had provision for support only for female widows. (1 Timothy 5:3—16) (See the discussion of roles in the family.) It is enough to say that the Scriptures decree leadership as the *burden* of the husband,

(Ephesians 5:22—33) complementary but not identical duties for both sexes, (1 Corinthians 7:3, 4) and charge the husband with the care of his wife. (Ephesians 5:25—33)

The male bears *burdens* the female does not including: leadership, teaching children, and loving (*agapee*) his wife. Paul commands Christian men that they seek a masculine role. (1 Corinthians 11:7) God directs that his people honor manhood and the masculine gender role. This applies especially to men. (1 Corinthians 16:13) Paul, the inspired writer uses *andridzesthe* (Imperative, present, middle, second person plural of the verb "make yourselves manly," My translation), "Quit you like men." This may have included the women, but the role is that of being like a Godly husband. Even today the continued respect for the church especially among men will depend in part on how they maintain this gender role.

How should the Christian regard gender?

- The genders are God-given roles, necessary to His will and to the world He intends. They are much more than sexual roles.
- Those who have either role must respect the roles of both sexes.
- Gender roles that are different, but complementary.
- Respecting the roles expresses honor for God the creator.
- God's Scriptures challenge Christians to the best expression of the roles God has given.
- This is another area in which Christians must not be "pressed into the mold" (Romans 12:2) of either custom, or current society, but rather each Christian should develop his/her Christian life by "renewing the mind" though the study of God's Word.
- The current advocacy of gender neutral roles comes from sources that usually advocate a sexual and/or family life style that violates Christian values.
- Both genders must give high honor to both roles. They reflect the will of the Creator and the design of the Creator for His Son and His Church.

CHAPTER 10

WEALTH: MATERIAL/SPIRITUAL

his chapter may be one of the most significant ones in this survey of Christian World View. Harley Swiggim, author of the Bethel Series, remarked in a workshop in Madison Wisconsin in the late 1960's that "The most difficult problem facing the one who preaches to a congregation is that nine of ten of those he speaks to are secularists and one in ten is a Christian." If that was true in the 1960's it may be even worse in the twenty-first century.

Jesus seldom mentions pagan gods. He does mention Beelzebub and one other, "Mammon." His statement is that "Ye cannot serve God and mammon." (Matthew 6:24) The Greek word He used, *mamona* is defined in Bromley (1985) as earthly goods and indicates that it comes from "the thing in which one trusts." It only appears in four statements of Jesus. (Matthew 6:24; Luke 16: 9, 11, 13) In Luke Jesus calls it the "mammon of unrighteousness," in the first two statements and again says "Ye cannot serve God and mammon." (Luke 16:9) It is interesting to note that the word translated "cannot" is actually that which indicates the "lack of power to accomplish, inability."

Paul, particularly in Romans contrasts living in "the flesh" with living in "the spirit." The expression "flesh" is a metaphor for a life that seeks first material and physical things. (One very popular version translates this "sinful nature" but neither sinful nor nature are in the word. Are the translators "stretching it a bit" to create "proof texts" for their biases?) The expression "spirit" refers to that life where the spiritual and eternal are the important and lasting things.

How Should the Christian Regard Wealth?

He Should Realize Its Dangers.

The Christian should view wealth with caution. The Scriptures tells us, "And the rich, He (God) hath sent empty away". (Luke 1:53) Luke 6:24 says "woe to you that are rich," other passages say that it is difficult for a rich man to enter the kingdom. (Matthew 19:23—26, Mark 10:23—27, Luke 18:24—27) In each case the Scriptures indicate that with God it is possible. First Timothy 6:9, 10; 17—19 warns against the temptations of riches and gives directions to those that have them urging them to they be "rich in good works, that they be ready to distribute, willing to communicate, laying up in store for themselves a good foundation against the time to come.". James (1:10, 11; 2:5, 6; 5:1) in particular pronounces woes on the rich.

The Christian should realize that riches are deceitful, (Matthew 13:22, Mark 4:19) and that those with riches or who trust in them have great difficulty in entering the kingdom. (See the last paragraph.) In Luke 8:14 in the parable of the sower, Jesus indicates that the seed that fell among the thorns represents those that are choked "with cares and riches and pleasures of this life and bring no fruit unto perfection." The Christian should be sure (1Timothy 6:17) that he is not one of those rich who are high minded (The word *hupsalophroneiv* is defined by Moulton (n.d.) as "to have lofty thoughts, be proud, overweening, haughty,") or set their hopes on the uncertainty of riches rather than on God. This is Paul's ongoing and personal command to anyone who is rich. The two things that the Christian who is rich must avoid are pride as if this gift of God were a personal virtue, and placing his trust in the riches.

Probably the most important principle is stated in 1 Timothy 6:10 "For the love of money is the root of all kinds of evil; which some reaching after have been led astray from the faith and have pierced themselves though with many sorrows." The word translated "love of money" combines the word for "affection or friendship" with the word for silver or money.

He Should Realize Its Potential for Good.

In the early church at Jerusalem Acts 4:32 tells us, "And the multitude of those that believed were of one heart and soul; and not one of them said that ought of the things which he possessed was his own; but they had all things common." This was not communism, but a spiritual attitude expressed within personal freedom. Ownership is recognized in such passages as Luke 16:11, 12. On the other hand the Christian is not his own according to 1 Corinthians 6:19, 20. The Christian rather has been bought with a price, so the Christian is to glorify God in his body. First Corinthians 13:5 says that love does not seek its own. Second Thessalonians 3:12 says that men should "with quietness ...work and eat their own bread."

What Should the Christian Regard as True Wealth?

Jesus teaches that His teaching and God's grace are the true riches. These are those which may be "laid up in heaven" where moth, rust, thieves, the stock market, the exchange rate or the price of commodities can not affect them. (Matthew 6:19, 20) The non-material treasures (knowledge and wisdom) are hidden in Christ (Colossians 2:2, 3), so the scholar should look there for his intellectual treasures.

What Is the Relationship Between Wealth and Security?

Riches do not give security, as 1 Timothy 6:17 says they are uncertain. The possession of riches may be a negative factor to spiritual life. (Luke 8:14) (Mark 10:17—27) The Christian should put his trust in God's provision and accept his grace. Jesus sent out his disciples as his messengers without providing money in the preaching of the "good news" during His ministry.

Steward and stewardship (*oikonomos*) have very few mentions in the New Testament except as Christ's followers were to be stewards of God's grace and in parables. First Peter 4:10 speaks of it saying "according as each hath received a gift, ministering it among yourselves as good stewards of the manifold grace of God;" This states an essential principle, Possessions are simply that which the grace of God has placed at our disposal but of which he requires that we be good stewards." (These things actually still belong to God.) "Possessions" in this sense occurs only in Acts 2:45 when the early Christians shared their possessions. We have the word in regard to Ananias and Sapphira with the warning as to deceit regarding possessions.

How Should the Christian Respond When Others Ask for Help?

In the first century church Christians did not consider their possessions as their own, but rather as something to be freely shared. (Acts 4:32—37) Jesus taught that the one asking a loan should not be rejected (Matthew 5:42) and that (Luke 6:30, 34, 35) and His followers were to be very little concerned with whether loans were repaid, and not refuse to lend to a "poor credit risk."

Principles for the Christian World View

1. The Christian should look at material wealth with caution, knowing it often is a source of evils, particularly separation from God.
2. The Christian should seek the true wealth which is in the non-material treasures which God makes available and which may be "laid up" eternally.
3. Material riches are not a source of security.
4. Possessions are simply that which the grace of God has placed at our disposal but of which He requires that we be good stewards.
5. The Christian will make use of material wealth as a tool, and will not waste it. Jesus commanded that even the broken pieces after the feeding of the 5000 were to be preserved.
6. The Christian will see material wealth as a resource for accomplishing God's purposes, but it is neither eternal nor indispensable.

7. Possession of wealth will not produce pride, but rather an increased sense of the weight of responsibility as God's steward.
8. The Christian will be generous in sharing his wealth with others. (Matthew 5:42, Luke 6: 30, 34, Acts 2:44, 45, 4:32—37)

CHAPTER 11

LEADERSHIP, POWER, FREEDOM

Leadership

*I*n life and in the church the role of leader constitutes a difficult but essential element in human relations. Leadership in God's economy is dramatically different from the understanding of it in the world. Kevin Leman (Leman) took the role of the shepherd as his model for teaching industrial managers how to manage their businesses. In the book it was revolutionary, but very successful. The scriptures frequently use the role of the shepherd as the model for leadership.

Jesus the Model

Jesus described His leadership as that of the "good (*kalos)* shepherd." (John 10:11—16) Hebrews 13:20 calls Jesus the "great shepherd of the sheep". I Peter 2:25 calls Jesus "the Shepherd and Bishop of your souls." The word translated bishop (*episkopos* footnote "overseer,")* (Thayer defines this word as "a man charged with the duty of seeing that things to be done by others are done rightly, curator, guardian, superintendent, overseer.) along with the word shepherd are two of the four terms which along with teacher and elder are used interchangeably as respects the leadership of the church.

What then is a good (*kalos*) shepherd? In John 10:11—17 states that the good (*kalos* – useful, beautiful, ethically right) shepherd has at least these characteristics:

1. He will lay down his life for the sheep. (Verse 11)
2. He will defend them against wolves. (Verse 12)
3. He knows his sheep and the sheep know him. (Verse 14)
4. He will cause the flock to grow. (Verse16)
5. The sheep hear (obey) his voice. (Verse 16).

In some ways the twenty-third psalm describes Jesus. The Psalmist indicates these roles.

1. The shepherds provides for the needs of the sheep.
2. He cares for their injuries.
3. He protects and brings them back when they stray.

The contemporary culture at the time of Jesus gives us two other characteristics of shepherds.

1. They are not those who look for praise of men. Shepherds were social outcasts.
2. Shepherds never drove their sheep. One man visiting Palestine asked a man who drove some sheep if he was incorrect in this statement. The man said he was correct. "Then why are you driving your sheep." "I'm not a shepherd I am a butcher." This is something the elder (shepherd/teacher) should consider carefully.

Another aspect of Jesus as a leader is that of the suffering servant in Isaiah 53. The prophet describes all that He suffered to be our great high priest (Hebrews 9:26—28) and the captain of our salvation. Hebrews 2;10 says of Him "For it became him, for whom are all things, and through whom are all things, in bringing many sons unto glory, to make the author (Captain) of their salvation perfect though sufferings."

On the other hand there is no compromise in Jesus as the leader. He says "I am the way... no man comes to the Father but by me." (John 14:6) This must be understood in the context of Jesus' role as the suffering servant. Christians and their leaders must take their cross and follow Him. (Mark 8:34—38)

The Characteristics of Acceptable Church Leaders

The first and controlling characteristic of these leaders in the church or home is that they vigorously obey the two most basic commandments, love of God and love of their neighbors. (Matthew 22:37—39, Mark 12:30, 31) The word translated "love" (*agapee)* refers to the result of a decision in which the person commits himself to do what he sincerely believes the best for the one loved. We have two lists of additional qualities needed for the elder/overseer (bishop) in the church. They are familiar and found in 1 Timothy 3:2—7, and Titus 1:7—9. These are available and easily understandable, though some dispute some details. (These disputes are beyond our purposes.) First Peter 2:21 extends this to the requirement that the leader follow Jesus "His steps." This makes all we have said about Jesus applicable to the role required of the leader in home and church.

The Characteristics of Acceptable Leaders In the Home

All that we have said about Jesus as the ideal leader applies to the leadership of the home. We also have two basic passages that deal with this issue. They are Ephesians 5: 22 through 6: 4, and Colossians 3:18—21. In both passages the leader (father) is *commanded* to love his wife. This is *agape*e the love described in the last paragraph. The wife is *commanded* to submit herself to her husband. She is not coerced into this decision. She does it as an act of obedience to God, *not* her husband. The word translated "be subject" (Ephesians 5:22, 24) is a military word referring to the relationship of a soldier to his superior. He obeys the superior in loyalty to his country not because the superior is better than he is. The wife accepts the position in loyalty to God, not to her husband. The verb in these cases always appears in the middle voice. It is something the person voluntarily does to or for herself.

Children are told to obey their parents, but their fathers are:

a. Not to provoke them to wrath,
b. To nurture them in the "chastening and admonition of the Lord," (Ephesians 6:4)
c. Not to discourage them.

The motive for the obedience of the children is an effort to please God.

Limitations

Not everyone who claims leadership is to be granted that role. John (1 John 4:1) urges the Christian to "prove the spirits, whether they are of God." He goes on in 2 John 10 in saying "If any one cometh unto you, and bringeth not this teaching, receive him not into your house, and give him no greeting"

The Attitudes of the Follower Toward God's Appointed Leaders

First, the followers are to respect the leader. (Ephesians. 5:33) They are to follow as their service to a more important leader. (God) (Ephesians 5:22) They are expected to give a certain gratitude to the leader. (Hebrews 13:7, 17 and 18)

How Then Should the Christian Look at Leadership?

Christians should approach leadership in harmony with the descriptions of leaders given in Scripture and, if they are leaders, fulfill the Biblical characteristics of approved leaders. Notice there are some things missing from these descriptions of leaders that are most often found in the human view of leadership. The elements in Christian leadership include the following:

•   The leaders are servants, not the ones served.
•   The leaders do not seek power nor take pride in their position. It is a burden they must carry because of God's decision.
•   They never drive their sheep.

- The leader commits himself (*agapee*) to the best interest of the persons served.
- Leaders and those served are friends as were Jesus and His apostles. (John 15:15)
- The leader is willing to suffer for the sheep.
- Those who follow are of no lower rank or lesser privilege, except as they accept the leadership of the leader.
- The leader must have good character.
- The proper response to a good leader is gratitude.
- God has appointed some leaders who are to be followed and the person not following them disobeys God. These include Christ, the Apostles, good Church leaders, husbands, and parents.
- A good leader never asks a follower to do anything contrary to God's will.
- The Christian should take great care in selecting the leaders he follows. (1 John 4:1; 2 John 9-11, 3 John 9-12)
- Like the shepherd, the leader knows his sheep; they know him and follow voluntarily.

Power

The Christian has little interest in his own personal powers. His focus is on the power of God as God grants that power to us, especially through the Gospel. (Romans 1:16) It is true that God gives certain powers as He sees they are needed. The Apostles had the power to do the works of an Apostle. Today, that power is transmitted to us through the Word. In the New Testament 4 Greek words are translated by the English word "power." These words are: 1) *dunamis* – ability, power, 2) *exousia* – privilege, authority, 3) *ischus* – strength, force, and 4) *kratos* – strength, power. (Young) The Christian sees all authority (a form of power) as ultimately from God. (Romans 13:1, Matthew 28:18)

Christ gives to Christians certain powers. In Eden God gave man the power of choice. (Genesis 2:16, 17) God grants the power, (John 1:12) in the sense of "authority" ("right") to become children of God depending on our faith. God has always made His power available to His followers as fitted His purposes and was needed. The source of power to deal with all the problems of life is God who gives it in our weakness. The Christian attitude toward personal power should follow the example of Paul. For Paul, God's power was made perfect in weakness. (2 Corinthians 12:9 and 10) As Jesus came as the "suffering servant." Christians are to follow His example which makes glory in power or power as a major goal in life inappropriate to them. Jesus gives us an indication of the approved pattern of the power within the church in Mark 10:42—45 when He says "whosoever would become great among you, shall be your minister (*diakonos* – servant, steward*)* and whosoever would be first among you shall be the servant (*doulos* - slave*)* of all."

The scriptures caution us that false prophets have powers even to perform "lying" wonders. (2 Thessalonians 2:9) We should test the spirits of any teachers to see if they are of God. (1 John 4:1) They must agree with the revelation given, in this case the inspired New Testament. (1 John 4:2, 3)

Freedom

Christianity by its very nature includes freedom and liberty. Jesus came with a message promising true freedom. (John 8:32, 36) Second Corinthians 3:17 tell us that "where the Spirit of the Lord is there is liberty." James 1:25 and 2:12 calls the law of Christ the "law of liberty." Freedom from sin and its curse is the most important freedom and is given to Christians. (Romans 6:18 and 22) Paul in Romans 8:21 speaks of Christians having the "liberty of the glory of the children of God."

On the other hand Christian liberty constitutes one of the most difficult elements in the Christian life to handle. Paul says in 1 Corinthians 10:23 "All things are lawful but not all things are expedient." First Peter 2:16 and Galatians 5:13 warn that the Christian must not use his liberty as an excuse for wickedness. Paul speaks of the limiting of liberty for the sake of others in 1 Corinthians 10:29—33 and in Romans 14, 15. Notice in these chapters Paul seems to indicate that the strongest Christians are those with the fewest prohibitions.

The Christian, therefore, should see his life as a Christian as one having a greater liberty than any one who is not a Christian. He will see that that liberty extends to nearly everything. On the other hand he will know that he must use that liberty honestly and responsibly. He will not use it as a means for excusing that which he knows (or even feels) is sin. (Romans 14:23) He will accept limiting of his freedom for the sake of others less strong than himself. (Romans 14:20, 21) This is the work of Christian *agapee* (commitment to the best interest of others, though it cost us something) the most basic Biblical law concerning human relations.

CHAPTER 12

WHAT IS DEATH TO THE CHRISTIAN?

*T*he issues concerning death for the Christian seem to include at least the following. What shall the Christian expect as to death and life? What do we know about life after death? What problems may the Christian have to face as to life and death? And finally, what procedures are appropriate for the event of death?

What Should the Christian Believe About Death?

The Scriptures contain a number of references to death as relates to the Christian. In John 8:51, Jesus says, ""Verily, verily, I say unto you, If a man keep my word, he shall never see death." In Romans 8:2, 6 Paul assures us that we are not ruled by death and Hebrews 2:15 tells the Christian that he is not under bondage to fear of death. Romans 8:38 assures us that death cannot separate us from God's love. In fact in 1 Corinthians 15:25, 26, Paul assures us that God will abolish death. Second Timothy 1:10 say that Christ has abolished death. This may seem to be a contradiction, except that Paul indicates that the end of death is so certain in 2 Timothy that it can be looked upon as accomplished.

The Christian life begins with a death to sin and the secular world (Romans 6:3—5) in Christian baptism. After this death has no dominion. First John 3:14 tell us that in Christ we have "passed out of death into life." James 5:20 tells us that if we convert a sinner, we have "saved a soul from death."

As the Christian approaches death of his body his attitude like Paul's (Philippians 1:21—24) should be "to live is Christ to dies is gain" and that to be with Christ is "very far better." (Like Paul, he should still be concerned that he is not needed to "abide...for your sake.") He also sees it as a time when he has "finished the course" (2 Timothy 4:7, 8) and when he expects the "crown of righteousness (or justification)" since he has loved and still loves (Greek perfect tense) Christ's appearing. (My translations). ["Fought the good fight" and "finished the course" are also perfect tenses which indicate something that happened in the past and is still important in the present.]

What Should the Christian Believe About Life?

Two words are translated with the English word "life." The first, *pseuchee,* is translated as life about 40 times and as soul about 80 times. The other word *zoee* is always translated "life" and appears about 140 times, with John, the most frequent user, using it in the gospel about 38 times. The two words seem to be used interchangeably for that which is life in the human being.

The references include these.

- Life is the goal of this life for the saved. (Matthew 7:14)
- It is eternal for the Christian. (Matthew 19:16; 25:46, Mark 10:30, Luke 18:30, and John 3:15, 16)
- The Christian already has this life. (John 3:36; 5:24; 25; 6:47, and 1 John 3:14)
- The Christian is to bear fruit to it. (John 4:36)
- Christ gives it. (John 10:10, 28)
- Jesus personifies it. (John 14:6, Acts 3:15)
- Repentance is required to receive it. (Acts 11:18)
- Becoming a Christian results in it. (Romans 6:4, 22)

- The goal of the Christian life is to magnify Christ by life or by death. (Philippians 1:20)

What Should the Christian Believe About Life After Death?

There is at least for a time a life after death for both the saved and the lost. (Matthew 25:34, 41, 46) John 14:2 and 3 tell us that Jesus has gone to prepare a place so that we (Christians) may be with Him after death. First Thessalonians 4:17 assures us that those Christians who die will rise and along with the living Christians will be "caught up in the clouds, to meet the Lord in the air; and so shall we ever be with the Lord." On the other hand those that "know not God, and to them that obey not the gospel...shall suffer punishment, even eternal destruction from the face of the Lord". (2 Thessalonians 1:8 and 9) Revelation 20:10, 14 and 21:8 describe this as the second death and a lake of fire. The fourteenth verse says "And death and Hades were cast into the lake of fire. This is the second death even the lake of fire."

The time references deserve some comment here. The Greek word *aion, aionos* may be translated, "1. age, a human life time, life itself, 2. an unbroken age, perpetuity of time, eternity b. in hyperbolic and popular usage" " from the most ancient times, by metonymy the world, the universe." (Thayer) (Thayer devotes 2 and ½ two column pages to the definition.) Bromley (He uses 1 and ½ single column pages.) cites as the contemporary non-Biblical use "a. vital force, b. lifetime, c. age or generation, d. time, and e. eternity." (Bromley) It implies an age, and when plural a series of ages. (Bromley) My experience with the Greek language indicates that the Greeks were very slow to speak in absolutes. This applies to the word "all" *pas, pantos* rather clearly when "all" refers in most instances to an understood group, not the universe. It may be that the word "final" may at times express the intended idea.

Theologians debate the fate of the lost. The traditional view (especially of the Roman Church) is that the fate of the lost is unending torment through unending time. For those not quite so lost they have an intermediate place called purgatory where sinners spend enough time to pay for their sins, then are admitted to heaven,. This is only for those "baptized." My study finds that the fate of the lost is "destruction" in every reference. The only place we have variance in punishment is

Luke 12:47, 48. The story of the rich man and Lazarus (Luke 16:22—26) is the only glimpse we have into the life of the unsaved, and this gives no indication of the length of time his torment lasted. Revelation 20:14 and 21:8 refer to it as the second death. A person has to be alive to be tortured. Death is when the body (regardless of whether it is cremated, embalmed, or not treated at all) returns to the elements from which it came. The idea that death may be equated with "separation" leaves much to be desired. It also makes the scriptures like Ephesians 2:1 and Colossians 2:13, which refer to spiritual death and James 2:17 which states that faith without works is dead much more relative.

The view of some writers includes an opposing scenario. Cottrell (Cottrell. *A Faith.*) notes that Russell Boatman (for many years president of Minnesota Bible College) held the theory that after a time of punishment, the lost would be destroyed. (Boatman) Ashley Johnson, the founder of Johnson Bible College held a similar position. (Johnson) The problem is that eternal torment requires eternal life (the reward of the saved). I find in the Old Testament that God always restricted punishment to a just level. For example the court was forbidden to sentence any person to more than 40 lashes. In the incident concerning Dinah and Hamor, Simeon and Levi are condemned for deception, but also for over-kill. (Genesis 34) Jacob (Genesis 49:5–7)) in his blessing, in effect, curses Levi and Simeon seemingly for these actions. That curse is carried out in history in that the descendents of neither son had any sure territory in the Promised Land.

We probably should add some comment on the *"near death experience"* as evidence of what happens after death. Maurice Rawlings a cardiologist has collected and recorded a number of this type of experiences (Rawlings). They appear to support both heaven and hell as determined by the religious conviction of the person experiencing the NDE. It should be remembered that they are personal experience and not documented fact, so the interpretations are just interpretations, but the book is an interesting one. Legally, none of these people died because they all retained title to their property and were still bound by any marriages.

Procedural Issues Related to Death

Mourning:

Matthew 5:4 says "Blessed are they that mourn; for they shall be comforted." This would seem to indicate that mourning is an acceptable activity and appropriate for Christians. Acts 8:2 says, "And devout men buried Stephen, and made great lamentation over him." Jesus seems to have participated in the mourning for Lazarus. (John 11:33—35) Romans 12:15 tell us "Rejoice with them that rejoice; weep with them that weep."

On the other hand 1 Thessalonians 4:13 seems to place a limitation on weeping when it says, "But we would not have you ignorant, brethren, concerning them that fall asleep; that you sorrow not even as (*kathos* – just as, like) the rest, who have no hope." Paul says in Philippians 4:4, "Rejoice in the Lord always; again I will say Rejoice." These are imperative verbs so are commands. Most Christians will seek to strike a compromise including both ideas. They will mourn for themselves and others, but will limit that mourning by the wonderful assurances they have in Christ.

One form of mourning is *funeral expenses.* Christians will differ as to what they believe are reasonable expenditures for funerals. They will certainly not go to the extremes of the Pharaohs of Egypt. For myself, I tend to believe that the Christian should limit these to what they can in good taste afford. I like the custom of making gifts to a Christian cause as a substitute for flowers, though I enjoy flowers. An elaborate funeral is often an expression of guilt for neglect of the person who died. Obviously the guilt will not impress the one who is dead though it may impress the less thoughtful among the living.

Burial Customs

This issue did not come to my attention until the widow of a fellow minister asked if there was any scriptural problem with cremation. I did some study and was happy to tell her that there was no scriptural teaching concerning how to deal with a corpse. (The family burial ground was in Oklahoma and they lived in North Carolina. The cost of transporting a casket was enormous.) In Jesus day they simply wrapped the body with spices to keep the smell down and put it in a grave or tomb. In Egypt they embalmed only royalty. Many of the martyrs for Christianity were cremated in the way they died. I talked with a funeral director and he said "eventually the grave will collapse and the chemicals used in embalming will seep out to contaminate the soil. There is no difference in the final result." Some Christians favor burial of the untreated body in a shroud alone allowing the natural decay to take place immediately. For most people of this is a matter of taste.

Organ Donations

I have never found those who object to organ donations on Christian grounds. There may well be a Christian action in making these parts available to make the lives of others better, so the practice may stand as a Christian act of service.

Summary and Suggested Viewpoint

These conclusions seem to outline what the Christian should think about death. A Christian view of death should include the following elements

- As a Christian he is already living in "eternal life" so death is simply an event when the transfer is made from one realm to another.
- A Christian will believe that Christ has prepared a place for him in a much better world.
- A Christian will be very concerned that others may not make the changes necessary and will find themselves subject to destruction. This will cause him to be very committed to the evangelization of the world.
- A Christian will have a deep reverence for the will of God and will attempt to follow any scriptural teaching concerning death, life, and immortality.
- A Christian will have a deep reverence for life as the supreme gift of God.

CHAPTER 13

A CHRISTIAN PERSPECTIVE ON HUMAN DESTINY

*I*n order to establish his "location" the Christian should have some commitments as to the destiny of mankind. This includes a view of the future of mankind as individuals and as a group. It also includes a view as to the object for creation and the ultimate destination of the world as a whole. This might be termed "eschatology" but that term has been taken so often to mean the study of theories about the end times of history as to lose some of its reference to personal elements.

I don't intend to deal with any of the theories. If you want to study "end times" I suggest you read Russell Boatman's book. (Boatman, *End Times*) I also intend only to state basic positions to contrast them with simple Bible statements.

All Mankind As a Group

Secular Theory

In today's world you have a variety of ideas about the "end of the world" and fate of mankind. The Evolutionist assumes that man will grow constantly better, but offers no future for the individual except good reputation. The Agnostic asserts that we cannot know what the future of mankind may be. The Nihilist maintains that everything will end in nothing

Christian Theory

Among Christian groups we have a very divided set of expectations. The early Restoration Movement leaders were mostly post-millennial. This was the view that the church would win the world, and some saw in the Restoration Movement, at that time the fastest growing movement since Pentecost, the hope that this object was now beginning to come into view. This is the reason that Alexander Campbell called his magazine the *Millennial Harbinger.* Today many have adopted a pre-millennial view. There are many variations of this view, but it is usually pessimistic about the success of the church in winning the world and assumes that there will be a return of Christ and one thousand years of His political and physical rule of the earth. This is variously timed with regard to a time of great tribulation. Most of these theories are tied to systems for interpreting Revelation. (Probably more books have been sold espousing various versions of these theories than about any other Biblical topic.) The third view is called the a-millennial view which generally assumes that the millennium (1000 years) spoken of in Revelation is a figurative expression and not a part of world chronology. It may also include the assertion that the "millennium" is the age of the church; therefore, we are living in it now.

A fourth view, which we will come back to with regard to individuals, is the theory of John Calvin. He maintained that everything of end time had been decided and planned before the creation began, with the inhabitants of the new world already named before creation and God's grace limited to that group sometimes said to contain 144,000 people. Calvin considered his *Institutes of the Christian Religion* divinely inspired and many of his followers grant them authority equal to or superior to the New Testament. (*Carson-Newman*) Others, like some modern sects, maintain the student can only understand the Scriptures within Calvin's teachings.

What does the Bible Say?

The Bible says of the future that there will be persecution of God's people and a world getting worse and worse. (2 Timothy 3:1, 13; Luke 21:24—33) Remember that Paul wrote these things during the persecution of the church by Nero. In Luke the prophecy may be primarily concerned with the destruction of Jerusalem. This may be compared with Matthew 24. In Verses 3—14 Jesus foretells much tribulation In Verses 15—35 He foretells the end of the Jewish national existence and in Verses 36—44 He foretells the end of the world stating that no one, except God the Father, knows when it will be. In 2 Thessalonians 2:3 Paul warns that there must be a "falling away" and "the man of sin be revealed" before the consummation of the world.

First, then the Bible says there will be an end of the world of which Jesus speaks in Matthew 24:36—44. In the next chapter (Matthew 25:31—46) He tells that He will come in glory and there will be a judgment when the fate of the saved and the lost will be announced. In Luke 17:26—37 and Matthew 24:36—44 Jesus describes His coming in somewhat different terms but there is the same division of the saved from the unsaved and the fact that no one will know when Christ will return. Second Peter 3:10 describes His coming as "the heavens shall pass away with a great noise, and the elements shall be dissolved with fervent heat and the earth and the works that are therein shall be burned up." Mark 14:62 speaks of "ye shall see the Son of man sitting at the right hand of Power and coming with the clouds of heaven."

Acts 1:11 tell us that Jesus will return as He left. His leaving is described in Verse 9 "And when he had said these things, as they were looking, he was taken up; and a cloud received him out of their sight."

Even Christ did not know the state of the world at the end. In Luke 18:8 Jesus says, "Nevertheless, when the Son of Man cometh, shall he find ("the" in a footnote. The Greek test has the article.") faith on the earth?" This opens the very real possibility, ignored by most theorists, that Christianity may be erased from the world before Jesus' return.

This seems to be reversed with the assurance that some Christians would remain in 1 Thessalonians 4:17. (In this verse it is interesting to note some of the grammar. It literally says "afterward we (emphatic) the ones living and remaining together with them will be caught up in clouds into a meeting of the lord into air and thusly we will always be with Lord." (My translation) The Apostle seems to include himself and his readers as those living and remaining. Historically, that is not true. It does however reflect the point from which Paul was writing and if it had happened that day it would be true.

The book of Revelation has many references to the end of the world, but these are expressed in figurative language and open to so many interpretations that I prefer not to attempt to deal with them, until God sends an inspired prophet to tell us the truth about them. (This is what He did with regard to the Old Testament prophecies.) .

Paul in Acts 17:26 says of God "and He made from one every nation of men to live on all the face of the earth, having determined their appointed times and the boundaries of their habitation." This says something that Isaiah and Daniel clearly state. God is in control of the fate of all nations, though their people have the power to control their personal destiny. He determines their success and their demise. There is absolutely no reason to believe that He does not do that today and will until the consummation. He and He alone determines the fate of the world daily and the time and details of its end. As you look at history, you can see Him completing His plan. There is purpose and direction in the universe.

Of Individuals

Non-Christian Theory

The Evolutionist has nothing to offer other than that death is the natural end of all individuals and should be accepted. The Mormon looks to the constant improvement until the person becomes a god. The Hindu/Buddhist sees "nirvana" (nothingness) as the ultimate desired end of the individual. The New-Age thinker thinks of the end of man as constant self-improvement. The Muslim anticipates a bliss with 10 virgins to serve him as the reward of the faithful, or the martyr. The secular school, including most public schools, sees in "Charlotte's Web"

(White, 2006) the answer to children's questions about death. In the book the spider (Charlotte) saves the pig from slaughter, but when she dies "she lives on in her children." This combines the evolutionary view with something of the Nihilist view. I doubt that many thinking children find this a satisfactory explanation of death.

Of Believing Christians

In Luke 20:35 and 36 Jesus tell us that those "accounted worthy to attain to that world, and the resurrection of the dead" will be unable to die and will not marry. (Matthew 22:30, Mark 12:25) In John 14:1—6 Jesus promises that He is preparing a place for His saints where He will receive them when He comes and they will be with Him. First Thessalonians 4:13—18, Paul says the Jesus will take Christians to be with him. Second Corinthians 5:1—8 Paul states that they "have a building from God, a house not made with hands eternal in the heavens" and that we will "be at home with the Lord." Stephen in Acts 7:55 and 56 gives us a glimpse into this place. Hebrews 12:22, 23 describes the place as "the heavenly Jerusalem" with "hosts of angels." To the repentant thief on the cross Jesus described it as "Paradise" (Luke 23:43) and this term is used by Paul in 2 Corinthians 12:4. He says that there he heard "unspeakable words, which it is not lawful for man to utter."

What will the state of these redeemed in this New Jerusalem be? Matthew 5:12 and 19:21 promise great rewards in heaven. The first of these is eternal life. (This is promised or assumed in Mark 10:30; John 3:16; 4:14, 36; Acts 13:48, Romans 5:21; 6:22, 23; Galatians 6:8, 1 Timothy 6:12, 19, Titus 1:2, 3:7, 1 John 2:25; 5:1, 13, 20. Jude 21 .and many other references.) John 5:24 says that those who believe already have eternal life and have passed from death to life. This is the most commonly mentioned reward of the faithful, particularly in the writings of John. John 8:51 says that the faithful shall never see death.

The Scriptures teach that that life will be one with blessings. Hebrews 10:34 calls it "a better possession (in heaven) and an abiding one." The faithful desired a better country a heavenly one and that desire would be fulfilled. (Hebrews 11:16) Mark 10:21 and Luke18:22 promise treasure in heaven. Luke 6:23 promises reward in heaven. First Peter 1:4 promises an inheritance in heaven.

The final question is concerning the nature of being of the individual in heaven. Paul deals with this most extensively in 1 Corinthians 15:35—58. He says first that the person will have a celestial, not terrestrial (earthly) body. He says that this body will be spiritual, incorruptible, powerful, and "bear the image of the heavenly."

I read the New Testament looking for information about what the life in heaven would be like. I found only this information. I did not consider material from Revelation because of it highly figurative character. It may be that revelation's figurative character and the seeming silence are indications that our finite minds are not able to comprehend how wonderful it will be. A few years ago and article appeared in a magazine concerning a group of people in the Philippines who had never learned to use clothing, metal or fire. Suppose a missionary or sociologist asked one of them to go home with him to New York, and that person asked "What is it like?" Would there be enough common vocabulary between them to give the man from the Philippines an accurate idea of what to expect. Possibly our state is comparable to the man from the Philippines.

Who are the saved?

I found that the saved included at least the group described by the following phrases:

- those with faith and patience, (Hebrews 6:12)
- those that believe and are immersed, (Mark 16:16)
- those who take the narrow and difficult way, (Matt. 7:13, 14)
- those who repent and are immersed, (Acts 2:38)
- those who have been born anew, (or "from above") (John 3:3)
- those who have been buried with Christ in baptism and raised to a new live, (Romans 6:4)
- those who have believed in Jesus, loved Him and the Father, loved those He begat and have kept His commandments which are not burdensome. (Christians.) 1 John 5:1—5

Of the Lost

Two words used for the destination of the lost are Hades and Gehenna. The first is simply the abode of the dead and comparable to the Hebrew "*sheol.*" The second is a term referring to the valley of Hinnom which became the dumping ground of Jerusalem. Luke 16:23 says that the rich man was in H*ades* and was in torment. This is the only direct reference to torment after death. Many of the other references imply it with such expressions as "weeping and gnashing of teeth."

Jesus speaks of Gehenna (Greek *geennan*) when He warns of the danger of going there in Matthew 5:22, 29, and 30. Mark 9: 43, 45, and 47 record the same warnings. Matthew 10:28 warns men to be afraid of the one who can destroy soul and body in Gehenna. Luke 12:5 also records this warning Matthew 18:8 and 9 repeat the warnings in Matthew 5. In Matthew 23:33 Jesus warns the scribes and Pharisees that they will not, given their present actions escape the "judgment of hell." (footnote Gehenna, Greek *geennees)* James (3:6) warns that the tongue is set on fire in Gehenna.

Given that the destination of the lost is G*ehenna,* what is said about what happens to them in that place? Three words are used to describe these events. The first is *apollumi* which is defined (Thayer) as "1. to destroy i.e. to put out of the way entirely, abolish, put an end to, ruin. 2. to destroy, i.e. to lose." These are the meanings given when not symbolic. Bromley (Bromley) states that the literal use is "a. to destroy, b. suffer loss or lose, c. to perish, d. to be lost (not sharply distinguished from c)." Jesus used this word in Matthew 10:28 as to destroying both soul and body in G*ehenna.*

The second word is *apoleia* and appears in Matthew 7:13 when the "broad way" is said to lead to it, and Philippians 3:19 which say it is the end of the enemies of the cross (translated "perdition" in ASV). This comes from the same root word so the information in the last paragraph applies.

The third word *olethros* is used in 2 Thessalonians 1:9 which the ASV translates "who shall suffer punishment, even eternal *destruction* from the face of the Lord and from the glory of His might." Thayer (Thayer) defines this word as "from Homer down, ruin destruction, death." Bromley (Bromley) defines it as, "corruption, destruction, death." The final result of the unsaved is (Romans 6:21 and 23 and James 1:15) death. (The word *thanatos* is defined as "die, separation of the soul from the body, destruction.") (Thayer)

Boatman (Boatman) along with Johnson (Johnson) raise the question as to the contrast of death for the lost and life for the Christian. A person must be alive to be tormented. The Roman church has taught a system written about by Dante of heaven, hell and purgatory. In their teaching torment in hell is just as lasting as life in heaven. Is therefore the result an *eternal life for all men* with some in torment and some in bliss? What is death to the body? It is the end of feeling and return to the elements from which it came.

Who Are the "Lost?"

In various places the New Testament lists as lost or "not inheriting the Kingdom of Heaven" the following individuals:

1. those who did not assist those in need, (Matthew 25:45, Luke 16:23)
2. those who do not control their tongues, (James 3:6)
3. those led astray by eye or hand, (Matthew 5: 29-30; Mark 9:43, 45, 47)
4. anyone who disbelieves in Christ, (Mark 16:16)
5. the one who calls his brother a fool is in danger of it, (Matthew 5:22)
6. the hypocrites, (Matthew 23:29, 33)
7. those who take the broad easy way, (Matthew 7:13, 14) and
8. the one guilty of lust. (James 1:15)

In other places there are list of those who are "lost." First Corinthians 6:9—10 says "Be not deceived: neither fornicators, nor idolaters, nor adulterers, nor effeminate, nor abuser of themselves with men, nor thieves, nor covetous, nor drunkards, nor revilers, nor extortioners shall inherit the kingdom of heaven." Galatians 5:19—21 says "Now the works of the flesh are manifest, which are these: fornication, uncleanness, lasciviousness, idolatry, sorcery, enmities, strife, jealousies, wraths, factions, divisions, parties, envying, drunkenness, reviling, and such like; of which I forewarn you, even as I did forewarn you, that those who practice such things shall not inherit the kingdom of God."

The ASV translates porneia as "fornication." My lexicons (Moulton, Thayer) define the Greek word as "fornication, prostitution, whoredom, an unchaste female." Some modern translations translate it as" immoral." This could include any violation of a moral code. This is *not* a possible understanding from the context. This is sexual intercourse between unmarried persons. (Webster defines it as "illicit sex involving unmarried persons.") (Webster)

Philippians 3:18, 19 give a somewhat different type of list when it says, "Many walk, of whom I told you often, and now tell you even weeping, that they are the enemies of the cross of Christ, who end is perdition, whose god is the belly, and whose glory is in their shame, who mind earthly things." The current secularization of the church and the materialism of the church members might make this passage one expressing a major concern of Christians.

None of these sins is unpardonable. The person must simply accept Christ as his savior, repent of these things and ask forgiveness. Repentance may involve some restitution, a Biblical teaching often stated in the Law of Moses. When the person asks for forgiveness, after true repentance, in the eyes of God it becomes as if it had never happened, and the church and its members must follow the divine example.

CHAPTER 14

HOW THE CHRISTIAN REACTS TO SUFFERING ("BAD" THINGS)

L ife in this world has always involved "bad" things happening. Some of them are very difficult to understand. They include suffering from natural causes. This includes such things as disease, natural disaster, age and possibly some other sources. A second source of "bad" things includes things that people do. This includes such things as economic problems, war, and the actions of people.

Americans have lately had a number of occasions when the seemingly "crazy" actions of people have caused great sorrow, pain, and loss to many innocent people. Even worse may be the times when these events are sources of joy to those who perpetrate them, such as terrorists.

People have a tendency to ask "Why does a good God allow these things to happen?" Why does He not prevent the devastation of the hurricane or the tidal wave? Why does He allow these bad people to hurt the good ones? Why does cancer strike this faithful servant?"

The importance of the questions may be indicated Biblically by the existence of the book of Job. Karl Jung, a student of Sigmund Freud, chose to deal with the problem of human suffering by his work *An Answer to Job.* (Jung, 1954) I am not recommending the book, but its existence indicates the importance of the question. The thoughts here propose at least part of the answer as we believe a Christian should see it in the light of Scripture.

The Context for the Answer

Perhaps this should be in a conclusion, but the *first assumption* of the Christian is that God's viewpoint is infallible and beyond human criticism. Paul in Romans 11:33—36 has written, "O the depth of the riches both of the wisdom and the knowledge of God! How unsearchable are his judgments, and His ways past tracing out: (34) For who hath know the mind of the Lord, or who hath been his counselor, (35) or who that first given to him and it shall be recompensed unto him again? (36) For of him, and through him, and unto him, are all things. To him be the glory forever. Amen."

Our difficulty in understanding may be that *we stand in a very different perspective* than that of God. Perhaps it is a little as if in World War I, we are the soldier in the trench with a very limited communication and whose vision can only see the walls of his trench. God on the other hand is like the one in the airplane who can see the entire battlefield, and comprehend what is actually happening. From this great advantage He can see reality when we cannot.

One very essential element is God's insistence on *human freedom of choice.* It is often this freedom that leads to the tragedies. On the other hand for man not to have this freedom would be an even greater tragedy since without freedom there can be no responsibility and therefore no righteousness, and no faith. These are the elements which make accountability and our salvation possible.

Reasons for "Bad" things

The first reason for 'bad" things happening *is human sin.* A man, who spent much of his life as a drunk" became a Christian, a much admired leader in the church. He developed disease of the liver, and some said "Why does God let this happen to this good man?" His answer was to say fiercely, "Don't blame my God. I did this to myself. God promised to redeem my soul, He never promised to redeem my body." When men, even otherwise good men. do that which is wrong they cannot escape the result of sin. The faithful missionary who neglects his family is subject to the likelihood of family problems. The "workaholic" church worker can expect the results of that sin even though God may forgive him. The Christian wife who neglects her husband can also expect bad things. How much more will the sin of non-Christian certainly in the long run produce in them the "bad" things? After all Paul (Romans 6:23) says "the wages of sin is death;"

The "bad" thing may be *a punishment for sin*. The history of Israel and the inspired pronouncement of God's prophets abundantly demonstrate this cause for "bad" things. When God punished his people for their rebellion, idolatry, secular values, dishonesty and debauchery, it was not a pretty sight. The people, many of whom were innocent, were led away naked by rings in their noses, many to starve and die of thirst on the way to captivity, and those who survived went to inhospitable land with no hope of returning home. Why did God allow this? The captivity was necessary to produce a remnant who were free of idolatry to fulfill their national purpose. It was just, because for almost a millennium God had sought to win them and they refused. We have indicated that in a smaller way this occurs in individual human lives. God demonstrated in these punishments his control of history and His justice. You can see these things happening in Alexander, the Romans, Hitler, Stalin, and others. We have no reason to believe that God will not punish the sins of the United States in a similar manner. God's justice in this is shown in Luke 12:47 and 48 when the number of stripes is in proportion to the sin committed. God recognizes that it is impossible to punish a nation without the relatively innocent being hurt. Wars are not fought by those who seek them, and often profit from them, but by those who don't want them, against other men who don't want them. Victims of wars suffer as God punishes the wicked.

Even more prevalent is the *"second hand" results of sin.* The parents who sin with regard to each other almost inevitably bring harm to their children. The thief harms his victim. The liar or cheat harms those he deals with. The murderer does harm to his victim. One kind of thing that we often don't think of as a cause of "bad" things is the failure of someone to do what they should have done. If I fail to keep my car in good repair my wife may be killed in an accident because of it. If a preacher or teacher does not tell all about sin, people may be lost.

Don't forget, the *Devil is real.* It was the Devil who tormented Job. God only permitted it. First Peter 5:8 says, "Be sober, be watchful, your adversary the devil, as a roaring lion, walketh about seeking whom he ay devour:" I once asked a young adult class if they believed the Devil was a real person, and they answered "no" unanimously That is typical of our world and the church. It is not a scriptural viewpoint. Job's adversary was *real.* Satan (which means enemy) wants us to think he is not real, so as to better deceive us and lead us into sin. He may be the source of much of the "insane" behavior which brings "bad" things. He was the source of the demon possession in Jesus day. His other name "devil" means "slanderer" which is a practice of liars, and Satan fulfills both practices.

This leads us to another source of bad things, *human error.* The pilot who took the wrong runway in the Lexington, KY airport did nothing intentionally wrong. He simply made a mistake. His mistake cost his life and the lives of his passengers. If God had programmed us to make no mistakes we would be robots, and even those have electronic or mechanical failures. He would also have limited the freedom necessary for righteousness, faith and salvation. This can also be true of the weather forecaster, or the one who elects to avoid the warning of the forecaster who is right. These errors account for much of the tragedy in recent natural disasters. They also account for some of the environmental catastrophes. The Gulf of Mexico oil spill occurred because of human error in drilling operations. This type of error can occur in the practice of medicine, (Some say many thousands die annually because of malpractice.) counseling, and human relations in general. The same destruction of man's necessary freedom would result if God prevented these things.

Finally, there is the *natural disaster.* Human error may make these "bad" things worse, but there may also be that which we in our "crude, incomplete" science have not yet come to understand. Perhaps these natural forces are necessary to the proper functioning of our planet. We need to continue to learn so that we may cooperate with the true Master of the universe and not be hurt as He administers the affairs of the universe.

Good Results of Bad Things

When they happen we may see little that is good that comes from bad things. The Scriptures however indicate that the results may be very good. One purpose of the book of Job (Which we would not have without the bad things) is that Job learned something. Sometimes "bad thing" *teaches us something necessary.* Job 42:6 gives Job's conclusion "Wherefore I abhor myself, and repent in dust and ashes." What led to this statement is given in chapters 38 through 41. The basic answer is "Who are you in comparison with God, and who are you to question what He does?" Job's sin, which he repented, was *lack of submission to God.* (or a *lack of faith* that God would make it right.) Abraham holds God to His moral standard in Genesis 18:25 when he says "shall not the Judge of all the earth do right?" In the light of what follows God does right for Job. (Job 42:10—17) He simply needed to be patient with God. This patience is a product of faith.

In 2 Peter 1:5—8, Peter in a list of things that make us fruitful includes *hupomonee* (The ASV makes it patience, but footnotes it as steadfastness). It is defined by Thayer as "steadfastness, constancy, endurance." You don't *develop endurance* by having good things happen to you, but rather by the bad things that happen to you.

Peter says "for a little while, if need be, we have been put to grief in manifold trials, that the *proof of your faith* being more precious than gold...is proved by fire." (1 Peter 1:6, 7) In Chapter 4:12—17 Peter writes, "Beloved, think it not strange concerning the fiery trial among you, which cometh upon you *to prove you*, as though a strange thing happened unto you 13) but insomuch as ye are partakers of Christ's suffering, rejoice;...16) for if a man suffer as a Christian, let him not be ashamed; but let him glorify God in this name."

Personally, I identify with Job at least in this way. I have before me a list of seventeen times when things "went wrong" in my life including the death of a child, physical illness, cancer, being fired for doing right, frustration with job hunting (137 applications, 2 interviews, 0 job), denial of the Ph.D. by one university, etc. As I look back on them I have *learned* that when the Lord gives us bad things they often *teach us a lesson and/ or give us something better.* But I had to wait years to see that that was His plan.

Finally, Paul in prison writes (Philippians 1:12) "Now I would have you know brethren that the things which happened unto me have fallen out rather to the *progress of the Gospel* (good news)." Paul had been in prison for over two years. In those days the only food a prisoner received was what friends brought him. There was no heat, sanitation, etc. Yet he says his sufferings advanced the gospel. It has been said that "the blood of the martyrs is the seed of the church." When you look at the history of the church, you often see that bad things *eventually* have good results. Wycliffe' by his suffering gave us an English Bible. Luther's "bad" things resulted in reformation and even the first western system of universal education. David Livingston's sacrifices opened Africa for Christ.

How the World Sees "Bad" Things

I think we should take a look at how the world reacts to bad things before we look at how a Christian should react to them. There may be a contrast as to things the Christian should not do. The world *expresses its values* in how they react. When Princess Diana (a person with questionable morals) died the "media" spent hours and days "informing the world" of the "bad" thing that happened to her. About the same time Mother Teresa died. You would hunt in vain for more than a simple mention of the death of this one who gave her life helping the lepers in India. If there is a tragedy related to a sporting event or a political figure, the "media" give it exclusive coverage and repeat themselves "*ad infintum*". Regular programming is junked in favor of these repetitions. When Christians are killed wholesale by Muslims (It happens by others, but most of the time it is this group.) you have difficulty even finding out that it happened. I am now seeking a good source of information. This is in the light of the fact that in the twentieth century I am told more people were killed for their faith in Christ than in any of the nineteen centuries proceeding. It isn't "politically correct" to report these tragedies. When faced with the question of why these things happen, the reaction of the secularist is 1) I don't know, or 2) God can't be good and let this happen.

How Should a Christian React to "Bad" Things?

If the "bad" happens to him, the Scriptures give us guidance. If the Christian suffers because of his faith, he should *not think it a strange thing.* Peter 4:12 we have "think it not strange concerning the fiery trial among you." Verse 16 says "if a man suffer as a Christian, let him not be ashamed; but let him glorify God in this name." In Verse 13 Peter writes " insomuch as ye are partakers of Christ's suffering, rejoice." Paul in Romans 8:17 says, "if so be that we suffer with him, that we may be also glorified with him." In Acts 5:41 Peter and John were "rejoicing that they were counted worthy to suffer dishonor for the Name."

It may be suffering because of the evil of others, or resisting temptation, but Paul writes in Romans 12:21. *"Be not overcome* of evil, but overcome evil with good."

An obvious first resort of the Christian should be prayer. Paul in Philippians 4:6 writes, "In nothing be anxious; but in everything *by prayer and supplication* with thanksgiving let your requests be made known to God."

If the evil is happening to others a Christian will *get involved.* Paul describes the Macedonian Christians in these words concerning the offering to help the saint in Jerusalem, "how that in much proof of affliction the abundance of their joy and the deep poverty abounded unto the riches of their liberality. 3) for according to their power, I bear witness, yet and beyond their power, they gave of their own accord." (2 Corinthians 8:2, 3.) Christians reach out to help those in affliction with joy and liberality. This may be money, or it may in personal contacts, sympathy, encouragement, and even with humor or music.

If the issue is one related to government, though they must in so far as conscience allows obey government (Romans 13) they still will do what they can to oppose evil as good citizens. This may include seeking service in the political arena.

Finally, their faith in God will lead them to *seek good results* even from evil. Jewish tradition includes this story of Rabbi Akiba. The Rabbi was traveling and came to a village. They refused to allow him to enter. Akiba said "God means if for good." He prepared to spend the night in the woods. A fox caught and killed his rooster. Abiba said "God means if for good." His donkey wandered away and was lost. Akiba said "God means if for good." He tried to study (the highest form of worship to the Jew) but the wind blew out his light. Abiba said "God means if for good." He slept in the woods and the next morning he found that brigands had assaulted the village, killing all the people and leaving only ruins. He had said, "God means if for good." Afterward he said, "If I stayed in the village, my rooster had crowed, my donkey had brayed, or they saw my light I would have died at the hands of the brigands". I think that most of the time, after time has passed we can see a good result, at least in God's values, of nearly all the "bad" things we find in the world.

This discussion does not "solve it all." I hope it gives some perspective into which committed Christians can put the evil in the world and not let it "overcome" them. I do not want an "answer" which will not be an expression of Christian love and hope, as well as the love of brothers and the Christian family which Paul writes about in Romans 12:9—21. I also hope that Paul's exhortations in Philippians 4:4—9 will be very much a part of your "answer."

CHAPTER 15

BIOLOGY, A CHRISTIAN VIEW

C opernicus and some early scientists faced the problem of dogmatic statements regarding science from a theology based on primitive science. The Christian today faces the denial of logical thinking in order to avoid acknowledging the possibility of God as the author of existence and therefore science. Possibly Copernicus and his colleagues might be more sympathetic with Christian views than with the current orthodox dogma of what is termed science. I am not an expert concerning Biology. I have drawn upon the work of those who seem quite competent in the field.

Christians Reject the Evolutionary Hypothesis.

The Christian sees biology and the existence of the world as based on the acts of an intelligent creator. The evolutionary hypothesis rests on a theory that has never been demonstrated, and one privately rejected by some who maintain it as orthodox scientific dogma. (This statement is based on an article I cannot now document concerning the fight over what approaches to world origins would be required in Arkansas public schools. As I recall it stated that one of those who argued most adamantly that evolution must be the only one view taught also privately had published material doubting that evolution was possible.) It states that all of biology may be accounted for by chance, and that all living things came from one cell, formed by chemical chance. This is in spite of the fact that Darwin stated that his theory found it impossible to find answers to the questions of how intelligence or life came into existence.

The theory violates the Christian view of God and His universe. Some Christians have attempted a theistic type of evolution, but this questions the intelligence of the Creator or His ability to create, for if He has power of creation why would He use such an inefficient" way for producing the creation? (Noebel, p. 138) Natural selection is a blind and cruel method for creating human beings. (Noebel, p. 138) Evolutionary theory undermines the importance of the atonement Christ's life" and sacrifice produced by denying the origin of sin and the process of redemption in Eden. (Noebel, p. 138)

Science Demands a Creator.

Science demands a creator. The scientific method demands the assumption of orderly, specific, discoverable Laws. Science presents this as an indisputable demand. To consider all things fortunate accidents is to make this principle invalid. With that in mind those who observe living systems find in them a technological complexity far beyond man's accomplishments. (Nobel, p. 140)

The more man discovers the more he discovers design. The simplest living systems, bacterial cells, have characteristics like factories with complex machinery more complex than anything man has invented, and with no parallel in the non-living world. (Noebel, p. 140)

DNA makes lack of intelligent design impossible or the result of an incredibly longer period of time. (I am wondering if any scientist has calculated the time when the sun had cooled enough to allow the existence of life on earth and how long its energy will support temperatures allowing life on earth.) This still has to account for the creation of the ozone barrier which is necessary for life. Is there time enough after these events for the evolution of protein into DNA and then the production of all the life forms we know? It takes at least twenty different types of protein to produce DNA. When it has been produced it has a structure comparable to a written language. (Noebel, p.141) In addition to this, DNA had to be present in the first living matter. This is an irreducible complexity which demands design by a superior intelligence.

Evolution depends on spontaneous generation. Oparin presupposed a prebiotic soup that gave rise to life. Dean Kenyon, a biochemist, contends that life must have originated outside of nature and gives four arguments for the position. (Noebel, page 142) First the origin of genetic information cannot be spontaneous. Second, most attempts to replicate the conditions for chemical evolution result in non-biological materials. Third, there is no foundation for the belief that pre-biotic conditions led to forming amino acids. Fourth, there is evidence that ozone, which produces decay, existed in significant amounts in the early atmosphere. (Dean Kenyon, biochemist, in Noebel, p. 142) If there was no oxygen there would have been no ozone barrier and ultraviolet radiation would have destroyed life. Ozone and the existence of life must have originated at the same time. (Noebel, p.142)

The second law of thermodynamics makes creation necessary. This second law says that the amount of energy available to do useful work is always getting smaller though the total energy remains the same. (The first law of thermodynamics) Energy as heat is moving from available use into cold. (Noebel, p. 143) This, contrary to evolution, implies a progression from order to disorder. If you take the second law backward eventually you reach a point where the available energy would logically exceed all available energy and violate the first law. (The total energy remains the same.) There must be a beginning. The two laws imply a downward movement toward destruction, not upward as evolution. (Noebel, pp142, 143)

There are specific barriers in the gene pool that prevent creating new species. Science has never been able with mutations to break these limits. Wheat never becomes a fruit. In addition, most animal mutations are sterile. (Noebel, p.143, 144)

There are gaps in the fossil records. We do not find fossils of intermediate species required for the theory. The very earliest fossils include very complex forms of life. Science has not discovered life forms earlier than the very complex ones in the Cambrian rocks. (Noebel, p. 145). The discoveries have not included transitional forms. Many forms would be useless until fully developed. "Punctuated equilibrium" offers little help because it is based on the lack of evidence, and still has all of the problems of the original theory. (Noebel, p. 145).

Mathematical probability forbids the theory. Most scientific studies involve some type of probability. A probability required for rejecting the null hypothesis (This states that there is no difference and therefore the event could have happened by chance.) often is set at $p<.05$, or this could only happen once in twenty times if there were no difference (It happened by chance.). The probability in coin tossing of tossing ten straight heads by chance is $<.001$. Now what is the probability of any of the intricate units of DNA being formed by chance?

A Conclusion:

Creation requires faith. "Faith is not illogical belief or belief despite evidence; to the contrary, it but is acceptance of something which is beyond definitive proof. God is not visible or actually provable. The same is true of evolution. Thus there is no difference between religious faith and scientific faith except the source of revelation." (Baumstarck) Evolution requires more faith since it runs contrary to reason, science and history. It is desperately held to in order to avoid acknowledging the necessity of a creator and of God. The Christian simply cannot accept what requires such blind faith and immense credulity.

Observations:

The Christian view of biology might be summarized with the following seven assertions.

A. Creation was a result of a far superior intelligence, God.
B. Creation was planned.
C. The creation is moving toward a logical consummation.
D. The intelligence that planned and created the world is the Christian's personal Father and so his protector, supporter, and friend.
E. It is now the Christian's duty to care for the world as God's creation and for it and all of its creatures in harmony with the will of God.

F. The Christian sees himself as the supreme creation of God, having His image, worthy of the highest respect and protection, but still as a fallen creature needing divine forgiveness and assistance.

G. The Christian sees the work of Jesus as fulfilling the need for forgiveness and accepts the conditions attached.

CHAPTER 16

BIBLICAL ECONOMICS

There will be many sincere differences of opinion among Christians as to the relation of Christianity and economic systems. There are two principles with which we should begin. The first is that *no economic system can save mankind.* Only Christ can save mankind from sin and from themselves. The second principle is that *no economic system is perfect.* The fact is that no economic system is even pure. Every system has combined some elements from competing economic systems. The issue is the degree of each element.

The Scriptures and a Socialist Economy

Church at Jerusalem seems to have advocated or practiced socialism during its early days. Acts 2:44, 45.tells us "And all that believed were together, and had all things common: and they sold their possessions and goods and parted them to all, according as any man had need." Again in Acts 4: 32—35 we have this description, "And the multitude of those that believed were of one heart and soul; and not one of them said that ought of the things which he possessed was his own; but they had all things common...For neither was there among them any that lacked: for as many as were possessors of lands or houses sold them, and brought the prices of the things that were sold and laid them at the apostles' feet; and distribution was made unto each according as anyone had need." It also appears that during Jesus' ministry there was a common purse which Judas held, but this seems to be more of a company policy than an economic model. Even after the church grew beyond Jerusalem they made extensive gifts to the needs of others. Those in Antioch (Acts 11:27—30) sent aid to the Christians in Judea. Dorcas was one noted for charitable work and may, herself, have been one of the widows for whom the church assumed responsibility as indicated in 1 Timothy 5:3—16. First Corinthians 16:1—3 indicates a very significant effort for the relief of want in Jerusalem by the churches in Europe.

It is very important to note that that *all these were voluntary* on the part of *every* contributor. You must also note that they were instituted to meet special problems current at the particular time. Many in the Jerusalem church faced the loss of any family support. The church also assumed that Jesus would be returning almost immediately. Perhaps it is also important to note that problems arose within these charitable efforts. Acts 5:1-11 records one problem. Verse 4 indicates clearly that the persons who gave were under no pressure by the leaders to give. Acts 6: 1—6 records another problem which led to appointing men to supervise the care of the widows.

The Scriptures and Private Property

From the very first the Scriptures recognize private property. Exodus 20:15 "Thou shall not steal" clearly implies the right of private property. Private ownership *and stewardship* of property is assumed to be the proper state of affairs throughout the Bible: Deuteronomy 8:11—20, Ruth 2:7—11, Isaiah 65:21, 22, Jer. 32:43, 44, Micah 4:1—4, Luke 12:13—15, Acts 5:1—4, Ephesians 4:28. Very early in the giving of the law (Exodus 22:1—15) Moses writes details for God's people concerning the management of private property and protecting it. It even approves slavery for debt. Such passages as Jeremiah 32:43, 44 support private property. Even among the early Christians in Jerusalem who had all things common it is clear from Acts 5:4 that private property was assumed and honored.

From the very beginning (Genesis 3:17—19) the right to property stems from the duty to work. Proverbs 10:4 teaches that diligence in work should produce possessions. This does not mean an absolute ownership. A Christian recognizes God as the Owner of all things (Psalms 24:1) and man as individuals and a race is His steward. Every person is accountable to God for the use of whatever he has. (Genesis 1:26—30, 2:15) Every person is accountable to maximize the Owner's (God's) return on His investment by using it to serve others. (Mathew 25:14—30)

Conclusions Based on This

Only with private property can man be responsible for the use of assets to serve others. Noebel argues that private property (Noebel, p.291) discourages greed and envy, and causes men to accept the need to work in order to serve others. It encourages man to carefully use scarce resources. This is in harmony with Jesus instructions after He had fed the 5,000 (John 6:12) that the broken pieces should be gathered up and saved.

Industry As a Virtue

Scriptures that seem to support industry include (Proverbs 10:4, 14:23, Luke 10:7). Christian thinkers have seen that industry encourages economic fruitfulness. It also may be one means to stifle man's sinful tendencies. In many instances it encourages cooperation and the efficient use of abilities. Many also believe that it also builds the worth of the individual and individual worth is a Biblical teaching. Worth should and can be based, as Edgar Friedenburg (Friedenburg) contends, on *how* one is valuable, not an assumption of inherent value.

Social Justice

Does social justice require that each individual have an equal share of scarce resources? Paul seems (2 Thessalonians 3:10-12) to think otherwise when he restricts eating to those who work. Scripture never supports equal shares of resources. Leviticus 19:15 says, "Ye shall do no unrighteousness in judgment: thou shalt not respect the person of the poor, or honor the person of the mighty." The poor and rich must be treated the same in judgment, therefore any system that gives advantage to either rich or poor violates God's will and Biblical justice. God teaches equality before the law, not equality of income or abilities. Paul in Romans 2:11, and Peter in Acts 10:34 both bluntly and clearly state that God shows no partiality. The Bible demands impartiality in opportunity, not in results. Much might be learned from the Parable of the Pounds (Luke 19:11—27) and the Parable of the Talents. (Matthew 25:14—29) Both are parables in which the lord (representing God) gives His servants according to their abilities and rewards them in proportion to their use of those abilities. This agrees with Paul's statement. God is the source and demonstrator of justice, and the Scriptures show that justice.

Freedom

Experience demonstrates that capitalism grants men the greatest freedom of any economic system. Freedom is clearly taught throughout the New Testament as a blessing and God's intent for His people. (Some in the history of Christianity have been very unwilling to grant it to those who disagree with them, to the disgrace of Christianity. See the Museum of Christianity in Moscow.)

Freedom and economics have a considerable connection. Socialism requires counter-productive bureaucracies, a powerful central government to enforce the system, and extensive use of coercive power. The individual must sacrifice much of his/her freedom. It removes from genuine charity the freedom required by logic and God.

History demonstrates that for the most part major socialist economies have had little place for Christianity. Communist Russia and China were officially atheist. Post revolution France was atheist. England had a lifeless church when it moved to socialist government. Most of the English churches are open one hour a week and serve less than one or two per-cent of the population.

Even when Christian groups have practiced a socialist economy these have been short-lived and lacking in personal freedom. The Zoarites were short lived. The Shakers who were strong in mid nineteenth century are now extinct. The Amish have been much more durable and successful, but though they may exert some social pressure, their "helping" each other is voluntary. This freedom also appears among the Mennonites, a related group.

Wealth and Poverty

In our chapter on the attitude of the Christian concerning wealth we have recorded the condemnation of the rich who abuse that wealth. James is very vocal in this regard. On the other hand poverty does not always come from exploitation by the rich. Poverty sometimes results from oppression and exploitation, but Scripture also teaches that there are times when poverty results from other unrelated misfortunes: such things as accidents, injuries and illness. The Bible also makes it plain that poverty can result from indigence and sloth. (Proverbs 6:6—11, 13:4, 24:30—34, 28:19) I would include with this the violation of God's instructions for care of our bodies and an undisciplined life. Biblical teaching considers both of these sins.

In capitalism the wealthy create wealth and desiring to advance it create the means that multiply the goods and services, provide jobs, and raise the economic level. There must be risk taking persons (they could lose everything) who desert simple and comfortable living to make the effort to produce these services. In a socialist economy those who gain wealth tend to hide it and those unwilling to work tend to assume that the government owes them at least basic comforts. This results in oppressive taxation, and reduces national loyalty. Creativity and hard work, like the farmer who works his land, produce both better people and wealth. Paul's statement is good economic theory.

Implications for Christians

These understandings should have implications for the day-to-day living of Christians. Parents should include them in their teaching of their children. Their work activity and their political support should reflect Biblical conclusions relating to these observations. Their attitude toward others who differ from them in socio-economic status should be with the freedom of Christian charity. Their view of their own possessions should include considering them all God's blessings and all belonging to God, to whom they are stewards temporarily charged with their care. The parable of the pounds (Luke 19:12—26) and the parable of the talents (Matthew 25:14—30) support this as the teaching of Christ for Christians.

This will prevent possessions becoming a source of pride since they don't belong to the person. Loss of possessions will only be important as it might indicate a failure in stewardship. Possessions are God's gifts to be invested and used for God's purposes: charity, extension of the kingdom, fulfilling obligations approved by God. Possessions do not define how important or how wealthy the Christian is. These are defined by the person he is in God's sight. A good stewardship of these blessing of God demands thrift, careful management, and unselfishness.

CHAPTER 17

HOW SHOULD A CHRISTIAN LOOK AT HISTORY?

Someone has said that those who will not learn from history are doomed to repeat its mistakes. To learn from something like history requires a theory of "how it works" in order to decide where the learner is in regard to the information. What about history? How does a Christian see history as "working?"

The Alternatives

One theory holds that we are progressing in an endless upward path. This is a basic contention of the evolutionist. It has a distinct parallel in the view of the Mormon that we are making endless upward progress toward being God. It also finds an expression in the "New Age" movement. A *second* and opposing view holds that we are progressing in an endless downward path. The second law of thermodynamics seems to support this since it rules that all heat is moving to dissipation in cold. This could be a movement to oblivion such as the Hindu doctrine of "nirvana". A *third* view holds that we are going constantly around in circles. Toynbee's cycles of history illustrate this and it has sometimes been called the "squirrel cage" theory. We see it in the maxims, "History repeats itself" and "What goes around comes around." A *fourth* view, Nihilism, says that history is actually meaningless. It is not going anywhere.

In *contrast to these* Christianity says that history was planned by God and operates within free will, but moves from creation to a final consummation. In that consummation the whole creation will be changed into a new paradise in which those who have found God's favor will be so changed as to be perfect citizens. It further states that in this there is a plan, order, progress, a divinely ordered schedule, and a divinely planned consummation.

What Most Modern People Believe

In our day the most popular view of history is a form of secular humanism. This holds that history is a long story of humanity's progress toward paradise. At times the humanist seems to have difficulty in viewing history with optimism, and sees it as making its bumbling, immoral and hopeless movement to the future. Today the humanist holds that, if we use technology wisely, we can control our environment and solve all of our problems, reduce disease, prolong our life-span, change the course of human evolution and cultural development, and give mankind an opportunity for a more abundant and meaningful life. (Summarizing Nobel, pp 299, 300. He quotes these ideas from The *Humanist Manifesto II* of 1973). Today these thinkers are forced by their dependence on evolution to be optimistic. If evolution is always upward, and all reality follows the evolutionary pattern then history must be the march upward to a better world.

Humanism

Humanism in general denies that God exists, and says there is no room for the supernatural. Man is a speck on a speck of a planet, so really not important. To avoid nihilism he must assert perpetual progress. This leads to the whole host of attacks on the Bible as in any way historically accurate or important for an age which has "outgrown" it. The humanist first asserts the dependence of man on the environment that shapes him, then to keep some optimism asserts that man shapes his environment. thus making man the important factor in history. To support the function of man it becomes the idea that 'ideologies" shape history. They progressively become outdated since man's thought patterns evolve as he does. The humanist ideology of course is the most useful one.

Cosmic Humanism (New Age Thought) has some peculiarities. It maintains that mankind has developed religions which he then progressively outgrows. A major failing of Christianity is that it has dogma which is responsible, according to new age dogma (as well as liberal progressive dogma) for nationalism, racism, and feelings of guilt. Mankind has now outgrown all of these. In the end mankind will be "'absorbed into a Divine abstract," where there are no distinctions, no words communicated and —only the eternal unchanging "now." (Nobel, p.317) Some New Age thinkers project the appearance of a Master Soul who will show the way to the perfect man. (Nobel p.317) This sounds like the Mormons. When a core have the "new age" consciousness they will bring all mankind into a godhead. This sounds like 2nd. century Gnosticism. Therefore, the individual is a co-creator with history.

How Does the Christian See History?

Most Christians probably just assume history is history. They are not consciously aware that their Christianity depends for its authority on history. Either Christ is a historical figure and the Bible is a historical document that describes God's communications with man and records events in the life of Christ, or the Christian faith is bankrupt. (1 Corinthians 15:12-19) On the other hand if it is dependable history, then the Christian has a worldview that conforms with reality, and mankind already has the "salvation" which other forms put in the distant future. If this is true the wise man will look to Scripture to learn all they can about Jesus Christ.

It is at this point that the liberal (claiming to be Christian) makes his most consistent and determined attack on Biblical Christianity. He attempts to discredit the origin of the books. He attempts to discredit the authors, or deny that the stated authors wrote the books. This is the battle that came to this country particularly in the late 19th. century. The Biblical side was represented by J. W. McGarvey and his conservative contemporaries. Today an increasing number of those colleges which at one time firmly held to Biblical authority are adopting views very similar to the "higher criticism" of the late 19th. century. The attacks on Biblical authority today take a pseudo-ethical slant. They criticize Scripture for not conforming to 21st century opinions on such things as sex, gender, and its secular relativism.

The Bible and History

This is the central and critical question. Is the Bible what it claims to be and what conservative Christens have held it to be from the first century: a dependable, accurate account of God's revelation of Himself to man?

First we must deal with the *question of authorship.* There is little doubt today that the books were written by eye-witnesses. William F. Albright concludes that "every book of the New Testament was written by a baptized Jew between the forties and eighties of the first century A.D. (very probably between 50 and 75 A.D)." (Geisler p. 309) By the middle of the second century lists of books considered inspired appeared and by 120 years (Origen, 210AD) after the death of the last apostle, the lists are nearly identical with ours. From that time onward no significant changes occur in lists of the books, and it is notable that this agreement spans the whole of the Roman Empire geographically. The distance spanned by the Empire in "air miles" is about 6,000 miles and riding horseback provided the most rapid transportation. Written copies still available include those written on papyrus and on parchment. Except among the Jews literacy was limited. Even the Jews had professional writers called scribes. In spite of these problems, by the end of its first century the church had a group of twenty-seven books generally accepted by Christians in all parts of the empire as divinely inspired and a source of final authority. Only one book, Revelation, lacks this general acceptance. Only one writer proposed even one other book. This could only have been accomplished by divine intervention.

That intervention was available. The special miraculous gifts conferred by laying on of the hands of the apostles (Acts 8:17) included: (1 Corinthians 12:4—11) 1) the word of wisdom, 2) the word of knowledge,

3) prophecy, 4) discerning of spirits. These gave the ability to make divinely inspired determination of which teachers and writings were actually inspired of God. The life of the church included these abilities well into the second century, and therefore up to years very shortly before we have the formal lists. A student of John was the teacher of the author of one of the earliest lists. Therefore, the books included have the authority of divine guidance for inclusion in the lists.

Many make the objection that it has been *"warped by inevitable mistakes* of copyists"* in the transmission process. In spite of this theory The Dead Sea scrolls in all statements are 95% exactly as the oldest dated manuscript (980 AD) and the differences are chiefly those which appear in obvious scribal errors, slips of the pens or errors in spelling. (Nobel, p. 323) Archaeology has consistently and cumulatively indicated that the Bible is a dependable historical document. The number of documents that are important to the text includes about 17,000 and in these the variations at no point produce a significant change in meaning. Compare this to 12 for Homer.

Christ and History

Some writers including Albert Switzer (*The Quest of the Historical Jesus)* came to doubt that Jesus actually lived. On the other hand ancient writers accepted him as a historical figure. Josephus (a noted first century Jewish historian who was on the staff of the Roman army that destroyed Jerusalem in 70AD) refers to him at least twice. As early as 112 AD we have an account of His trial and death from a secular writer, Tacitus. As time moves on more and more writers consider Him and acknowledge Him as a clearly historical figure.

The central event in the life of Jesus, His resurrection, must be considered historical fact or Christianity loses any credibility. Even Paul asserts this. (1 Corinthians 15:1—19) Fair minded intelligent people who have sought to disprove it find that the evidence for it is overwhelming. Lou Wallace (an attorney and therefore well schooled in the laws of evidence) after seeking evidence to prove that Jesus was not a historical person, wrote *Ben Hur* which is a clear admission of the facts. The scriptures present a witness list that is indisputable. The apostles affirmed it as eyewitnesses at the risk of their lives. (Acts 4:21; 5:18, 12:1—19) Acts 1:21 and 22 establishes them as eyewitnesses of the ministry of Christ and particularly of His resurrection. History records that many times they faced threats and most of them gave their lives for the truth and authority of the things recorded in the books in the New Testament.

A Christian World View of History

A Christian based on these facts will view the history of the world and his own history with the following assumptions.

God is working things together for good to those who commit themselves to him. (Love – *agapee*) (Romans 8:28) (The ASV footnote states that some authorities read "God "worketh all things.") In the grammar of the sentence the verb, "is working" (Greek present tense) requires a nominative singular subject. With this verb suffix it would be "he". The antecedent must be the nearest preceding nominative masculine noun which is God. The tense also indicates continuing action, so His actions may be assumed today.

The following seem to be logical assumptions based on the evidence:

- Difficulties even persecution are the logical outcome of Christian faith, but cannot defeat it.
- History consists of the unfolding of God's plan which will result in the victory of His followers.
- The present is important as an opportunity to serve God in accomplishing that goal.
- The beginning of history cannot be a result of chance, or chance be the force that molds either history or its inhabitants.
- History has purpose. It is linear - moves toward a goal
- It follows that the most important thing in our lives is to assist in God's purpose as it moves toward His consummation.
- Christians today stand as a pivotal element in history. Their concern for the lost, commitment to proclaiming God's message, service to God and their fellow men will shape history as they move through time.
- The fate of nations, even our own, depends on the will and plan of God. (Acts 17:26-28) This is abundantly demonstrated in the Biblical history of the Assyrian, Babylonian, and Persian empires. (There are numerous mentions in the prophetic books.)

CHAPTER 18

LAW, A CHRISTIAN VIEW

*H*ow a Christian relates to law constitutes an important part of his life while on earth. The most direct teaching concerning this for the Christian appears to be the statements of Paul in Romans 13:1—7. In Ephesians 6:5—9 Paul gives directions concerning the behavior of servants. In some senses the Christian at the secular level is the servant of the state and these directions seem applicable.

The Source of Good Law

God has provided laws for mankind as well as the means for knowing them. (Noebel. p. 231) The Scriptures in James 4:12 states the "one only is the lawgiver and judge..." This statement does not make God the source of all law since some of it is corrupt and even evil. It does place the source of all good law in God Himself.

The effective central concern and source of that law should be God. When law centers in man it fails to recognize the image of God and God's right to determine right and wrong. We discussed this in our treatment of Axiology which includes the study of the nature of right and wrong.

If the origin of law, and right and wrong is man, then man can make law for himself as he wishes. This leads to disrespect for law. It involves the view that anything is permissible that man wishes. Legal standards then are tied to the mores of the current society. An all powerful state offers no positive standard for the making or the enforcing of the law, since it is relative to the wishes of those making it and perhaps their social group. There are many illustrations of this in history, and also of the inevitable autocracy, cruelty and evil that results.

To the Christian God is the ultimate law-giver. God reveals laws through general and special revelation. Some of God's law is revealed through natural sources. Paul in Romans two says that some do God's law without aid of revelation and become a law to themselves. (Romans 2:14) Noebel (Noebel) and others hold the theory that there is within man a conscience which causes him to know right and wrong. I question this since it implies that men inherit their moral information. I wonder if this fails to take into account the fact that "natural" law may be the law passed down from Adam and/or the patriarchs. God was obviously the first law-giver. Where is there evidence that He did not also instruct Adam in other of His laws? The universal existence of some laws argues for this. The fact that people are not perfect communicators of law will account for the differences among cultures, as well as man's sinful state. There are some things that are clearly contrary to the intent of the creator, and man has the responsibility to know and obey the creator's will.

God added to this special revelation of His will. Noebel (Noebel) and many conservative Christians seem to believe that the Law of Moses (from which the Apostles say we have been freed) is the divine standard. Note that Peter (Acts 15:10) says it was a burden we could not bear and Paul calls it a curse. (Galatians 3:13) Though we are not under the jurisdiction of the Law of Moses, it provides guidance (not commands) for determining the application of the "royal law" which James (James 1:25; 2:8—12) defines as the two loves (for God and neighbor) which Jesus stated supported all the law and prophets. Remember that these are *agapee, not* the English "love." We become new creatures in Christ and that reality grows more and more dominant as we obey the "royal law."

The Christian and Law (or Government)

The most direct teaching concerning this is Romans 13:1—7. In that passage Paul, the inspired apostle, writes, "I am ordering (third person imperative) every soul to subject himself (The middle and passive are spelled the same in the present tense so I chose here to translate it as middle.) to the higher authorities." (My translation) The Apostle orders every soul, so the subjection is a voluntary act, not coerced. The context indicates that these "higher authorities" are the civil government.

This Christian renders this subjection both from respect for the government, and because the government represents God. (Romans 13:5) This subjection will cause him to render the taxes, respect and honor that are due the government. (Romans 13:7)

The Christian is perfectly justified in using the civil government to protect himself as Paul does in his relations to the Roman government in Acts. (Acts 16:35—39, 22:25—29 and 25:11) On the other hand the Christian is not to use the civil courts for settling disputes among Christians. (1 Corinthians 6:1—7)

There is precedent (1 Corinthians 5:1—5) for having church courts to assist in enforcing Biblical commandments. Paul specifically (1 Corinthians 5:12) rejects the idea that these would have jurisdiction over non-Christians.

Finally, the work of the *episkopos* (overseer, supervisor, bishop) involves the use of law since Hebrews 13:17 orders Christians to obey them and submit to them because they have the duty of watching over the souls of Christians.

The Christian as a Citizen

The Christian will see God as the perfectly wise and perfectly ethical source of the best law. The Christian need not fear just laws because he is already committed to obeying the law of God. (Romans 13:3—6) In verse 4 this ruler is called *diakonos* the word we transliterate as deacon but which means steward (a servant with a given responsibility) and is used of most of the first century church leaders. In verse six the ASV translates another word *leitourgoi* as "minister" but that word is one meaning who serves as an intermediary in worship. It is interesting to note that only in verse two do we have the article with the word *theos* (god). It is a generally assumed translation that *theos* with the definite article (the) refers to the one living God. Other expression may be translated as "divine", "deity" etc. This may alter how you see some of the emphasis in these verses. It may be that Paul intends to indicate God, but the translation may be "a divine servant."

This brings us to a problem. The relation of church and state dominated church history from the fourth century to the reformation and in many places long after the reformation. Though Noebel may not intend, when he insists that the state encourage people and punish evil doers, (Noebel, p.240) that government should be the arm of the church to enface its law; for several centuries this was the view of the medieval church. History amply demonstrates that when government becomes the tool of the church to enforce its rules, almost inevitably men lose their freedom. For Calvin this meant that the civil government should imprison and take the lives of anyone who disagreed with him. His role in the death of Servitus is best known, his persecution of the anabapistists (all that practiced adult baptism) is less known. It is even more clear in the actions of the Roman church which perpetrated what may have been the worst atrocities to maintain their teachings. They have never in any way expressed regret for these actions. In fact they honor those that perpetrated these atrocities by naming their universities after them. The exhortation of Paul does not condone this miss-use of power by governments.

Christians, however, should seek, when they have a choice, men to govern who will recognize God's law in their work as legislators. These representatives should make laws within their understanding of God's nature and will. These are those who become God's servants. (deacons - *dikonos*) (Romans 13:4) They and their laws should be impartial as God himself. (Romans 2:11) When the Christian becomes such a lawmaker, it is his duty to study God's revelation for guidance. He must respect others as "made in the image of God." He must to the extent of his ability devise and maintain an ordered legal system. The example of Moses and Jethro is an example. The system should be equitable, showing no partiality. (Deuteronomy 1:17) He should not assume that every sin should be made illegal. This would result in an even more boated civil system. Laws should only be made to maintain and protect human rights.

In the administration of law, this should include, for the crime, that it be 1) a fair and just trial, 2) diligently inquiry producing satisfactory proof and 3) a verdict that is beyond all reasonable doubt. (Novel, p.

238) It is much better to fail to convict the guilty than to punish an innocent man. (Nobel, p. 238) In our country we have (contrary to some European countries) made the legal process a game in which it is often more important to "win" than do justice. Attorneys get and keep their positions on how many cases they win, not whether justice is done.

Paul's example would indicate that there are occasions when the church should go to the courts to 1) advance or oppose legislation, 2) to seek relief from the actions of men or social institutions. On the other hand the church should be very cautious in the use of the civil government to enforce its wishes. Paul (1 Corinthians 5:12) forbids the church judging non-Christians. We can learn from history that the union of church and state which has, as we have indicated above, been one of the disgraces Christians has brought on Christianity.

A Necessary Restriction

The Christian will see God as his first allegiance and his first source of law. He will obey God when God's commands conflict with those of human courts. This is clearly stated in Acts 4:19, 20 and Acts 5:29. He should be cautious that what is said of God's law is clearly a command, not an opinion based on human reasoning. Care must be taken to avoid divisions among Christians based on human opinions were there is no direct and clear scriptural statement.

Observations

The following seem to follow from this discussion. The Christian will see God as the source of law. He will evaluate the law in the light of revelation, but not expect the non-Christian to be a perfect administrator of God's law. He will seek to have those who are Christians as his lawgivers when possible, but will accept the law-givers God puts in place as a necessary factor for order. He will refuse to obey the law given by men if they clearly require him to disobey one of God's *stated* commands. (He may on occasion refuse obedience if it causes him to violate his conscience, but this is a very personal and complicated response.) This is complicated by Paul's statement in Romans 4:23 that "whatsoever is not of faith is sin." He will not use the courts to settle disputes among Christians, but may use his civil rights to the advantage of the kingdom.

CHAPTER 19

POLITICS - A CHRISTIAN VIEW

*M*uch of what might be said here is already included in the sections on "Law" and on Axiology under right and wrong. At this point we look more specifically at the participation of the Christian in government.

First, the Christian should have a respect for government as ordained of God. (Romans 13:1—9, 1 Peter 2:13, 14) He will see Jesus as the Christian's supreme king. God has always been concerned for good government. In the United States the structure has been described as "a democracy within a republic." Pure democracy is the autocracy of the majority. A republic provides protection and respect for minorities. How well the United States fulfills these characteristics has varied over time, and is probably not perfect today.

Characteristics of Good Government

The Christian will hold that government should involve a sensible division of duties so that no one will be forced to bear more than he can handle. This is exemplified in the case of Jethro's advice to Moses. (Exodus 18:19ff) He will hold that there is no one divinely appointed form of government. The form should serve well the purposes of government in the given situation.

The purpose of Government is to protect mans unalienable rights from the sinful acts of others. This simply promotes justice. To the Christian this is the principle reason for government. Noebel's view (p.266) and that of the Dutch Reformed church (Normative spheres as represented by Spier and Dooyevard) (Spier) include the following principles. The function of the government is to provide justice. The function of the church is to provide grace. The function of the home is to provide community. With these purposes forces in one sphere, should not meddle in the affairs of another sphere. Therefore government should not interfere with religious freedom, attempt to control family size, interfere with the education of children, or control the economy. (p. 266) On the same principles the church should not attempt to control the government. Abandoning these distinctions of purposes for trust in an individual or the state will result in an abusive state. Looking to the state for a utopia will result in autocracy.

Within the system, those involved should recognize that "absolute power corrupts absolutely." Therefore, there must be limits on the power of all elements in government. Each part should understand the limits of its responsibility, and stay within them.

Obedience to the State.

Obedience to a just government is a necessity to keep the need for governmental power at a minimum. When the government strays from its purpose it is the responsibility of the Christian to seek to correct this or he will be forced to disobey the laws. This may involve seeking political office and political action. These are more successful than civil disobedience.

On the other hand if obeying the government would result in disobeying God, then the Christian must disobey the government. (Acts 4:19, 20) This has always been God's requirement. In the Old Testament Shadrach, Meshach and Abednego obeyed this principle and God preserved them. (Daniel 3) Daniel defied the king (Daniel 6) and God preserved him. Peter and John (Acts 4) refused obedience to the council (*sunedriou* Sanhedrin). Peter and John (it may have been an even larger group of the Apostles) defied the government. (Acts 5:33–42) The insistence of the Christian that theirs was the only God and Caesar was not a god caused them to be classified as atheist and considered guilty of treason. This resulted in the martyrdom of many Christians. At a point it becomes the duty of the Christian to disobey the state, even if it costs him his life. Success is not the criteria of virtue, obedience to God is.

The Role of the Church in Political Activities

If the church knows a particular candidate well and believes him to be committed to God's way of life it may support that person. Teaching support or opposition to certain issues is often the duty of the church. As individuals Christians may lend financial support to those for whom they have confidence. Care should be taken that the views of *all of the members* of the church are expressed in these actions. If that is not clearly true, the church should leave the issues to the individual Christian.

Another aspect of the issue is the question as to whether the church should accept government support. This might come in the form of subsidies to colleges, and may even be involved in accepting tax exemptions. Those who support, even if it is government, almost inevitably exert some form of control. The experience of the church through the centuries rather dramatically demonstrates that when church and state develop intersected authority, freedom suffers, and usually it is the freedom of sincere Christians, not the established "church." Our government considers subsidies to students as subsidies to the college (See the Grove City College experience.) and claims the right to regulate these colleges.

Another aspect concerns the relation of the state and the home. The church may in some circumstances (as a body or as individuals) take legal action if the state seems to compromise the parent's role. This has special importance when the education of the child is involved. The church, or individual Christians, may feel compelled to have their own schools if the public schools teach as fact that which compromises religious commitment or morals. This may take the form of schools controlled by Christians, or home schooling.

Since we have no divinely prescribed system of government. (other than God as the general author) Christians can often disagree on issues.

The church must find a way of preserving the unity of sincere Christians, and still have clear moral and spiritual teaching.

Dr. Joseph Baumstuck suggests that the book, *One Nation Under God: a Christian Hope for American Politics* by B. Ashford and C. Puppalardo, (Baumstuck) has some valuable insights in the area of Law and Politics. I have not had occasion to read the book, but trust his judgment.

CHAPTER 20

PSYCHOLOGY AND A CHRISTIAN WORLD VIEW

*T*he Christian should understand that Psychology for many centuries was considered a branch of Theology. The Greek words *psuchee* and *logos* are the elements of the term. *Psuchee* is defined as "breath, life, soul." (Moulton) *Logos* is the common suffix indicating "a considered study of" using the Greek word, *logos,* which means a considered word as contrasted to the Greek word *hreema* which refers to casual conversation. Therefore, Psychology may be considered the considered study of the soul. Two forces caused the divorce of Theology and Psychology. First, the extravagant claims made for it in theology put it in disrepute. Second, students of Psychology wanted to make it a scientific discipline rather than a philosophical one. This led Welhelm Wundt to found a laboratory of Psychology which approached the study in the through the pattern of physics, and many modern psychologists consider this the beginning of Psychology.

Modern psychology is built on human theories of such men as Freud,

Skinner, Pavlov and Rogers. Though these are dominant thinkers in modern psychology, after completing a large minor in Psychology for the Ph.D. from the University of Minnesota, I am inclined to believe that Psychology is a source of ideas which when viewed in a Christian philosophical base are rather useful. It is interesting however to note that all of the basic theories of these modern thinkers were discussed in Athens about 300 B. C. (Britt) Christianity has survived and flourished though men held many theories that Christians cannot accept.

The Bible and Psychology

The Bible includes no systematic philosophy of man, or statement of his psychology. It does include in popular form an account of human nature in all its relationships. A reverent study can lead to a well-defined system of psychology on which the scheme of redemption is based. Great truths about human nature are presupposed in and accepted by the Old and New Testaments. The Scriptures emphasize things only learned by revelation and these are presented in popular, not scholarly, terms.

The Bible presents man as fallen, degraded, but intended to be raised, redeemed, and renewed. Biblical psychology against this background should have a logically consistent view of the life, and the life-destinies of the soul. (ISBN)

The Bible and Psuchee (the soul)

The Scriptures are silent on the origin of the Soul. They tell us that "and God formed the man from the dust from the ground and breathed into the face of him breath of life and the man became into a living soul." (Genesis 2:7) [My literally translation from the LXX] If Moses had been writing in Greek this would be very significant. The Hebrew word translated soul is defined by the lexicon (Brown, p. 658) as "that which breathes, the breathing substance or being, that which becomes a living being by God breathing into the nostrils of it, by implication of animals also, a living being whose life resides in the blood." It refers to the life, and is not specific as to more than that. The same Hebrew word used here for "soul" is used to refer to all kinds of animal life. It is significant that seventy of the most noted rabbis of the century before Jesus selected a Greek word *psuchee* that was rather specific to what we think of as the "soul" as contrasted to "life" in general. *Psuchee* is defined (Thayer) as "1. Breath, 2. The soul seat of feelings and desires, affections, aversions ...an essence that differs from the body and is not dissolved by death." (This is a very abbreviated definition. Thayer's discussion takes a full double column page.)

Job adds (Job. 33:4) the "Spirit of God hath made me and the breath of the Almighty giveth me life." The LXX translates this from the Hebrew to say "The divine spirit made me and the breath of the almighty (is) the (one) teaching me." Breath is rarely if ever is attributed to animals. Other Old Testament references include Job 32:8, 34:14, Isaiah 2:22, Proverbs. 20:27. In the New Testament key passages include these. In 1 Corinthians 15:44, 45 Paul writes, "It is sown a natural body; it is raised a spiritual body. The first man Adam became a living soul, the last Adam a life-giving spirit." John 6:63 states, "It is the spirit that giveth life, the flesh profiteth nothing." (Note: Some of these may be metaphorical of the soul.)

Church leaders have held two theories (*ISBE*) of the nature of man. Probably the most popular is that man has a dual nature. This includes body and soul, with spirit considered as a manifestation of the soul. My own word study indicates that soul and spirit are used interchangeably, but are not synonyms. They are linked together in such passages as: Luke 1:46, 47, Matthew 26:38, 41.

Another theory considers human beings to have three parts. This assumes that the spirit constitutes man's higher nature with the soul being his "lower" nature. This view is also supposed to be supported by Scripture. In the early church the three element theory found favor influenced by Plato but was discredited on account of the Apollinarian heresy. Apollinarius of Laodicea attempted to explain Christ's person by stating that Christ has the divine *Logos*, with a human body and the soul is the link between the two. The Divine *logos* took the place of the rational soul (spirit) in Christ. (ISBE) This tripartite theory is based on two critical texts. The first is 1 Thessalonians 5:23 and may be an example of Paul's frequent piling up of terms for emphasis. In Hebrews 4:12 it may be that the author was seeking to state an utter impossibility. To base an important doctrine on two isolated and variously understood texts is extremely dangerous. In these cases we must also include the possible instance of metaphor, not literal speech (*ISBE*).

In spite of this man is a unity in Scripture. It is clear from 1 Corinthians

15:37—49 and 2 Corinthians 5:1—5 that a body and spirit are essential parts of man both here and hereafter. The frequent tension between these parts is the subject of Paul's discussion in Romans 7:14—8:4. (I maintain that verse 8:1 is the answer to Paul's question in verse 7:24.) Psychic action is sometimes ascribed to all three terms. Neither body nor soul separated is a man. Both spirit and soul are used interchangeably, and the body is used to refer to human nature in general. Marais (ISBE) offers this summary of the scriptural position, "The Divine spirit is the source of all life. It is communicated in physical, intellectual and moral spheres. Soul, though identical with spirit, has shades of meaning that spirit does not. It represents the individual. By easy gradation "spirit" may stand for the abysmal depths of personality; while "soul" would express man's individuality in general." The terms also have considerable metaphorical use. Paul uses "soul" to emphasize the physical and mortal, and "spirit" to emphasize the immaterial and immortal.

What Is The Origin of The Soul?

Three principal theories have attempted to state the origin of the soul. The first, "Emanation," supposes that the human spirit flows spontaneously from God. This theory became mostly obsolete by the late fourth century. It was formally condemned by a synod held at Constantinople in the sixth century. Kant, Shelling and others (It was specially defended by Julius Muller.) revived it. The key scripture is Jeremiah 1:5.

The second view is Creationism which teaches that each soul is created by God *ex nihilo* at birth. The early Church favored this view. It was dominant in the east and advocated in the west. Later advocates included Scholastics, Roman Catholics, and Reformed orthodoxy. There is little support in Scripture but these verses are used by its advocates: Ps. 33:15, Zech. 12:1, Ecclesiastes 12:7, Numbers 16:22, Numbers 27:16, Hebrews 12:9 and Numbers 27:16. Some have sought to calculate the day during pregnancy in which the soul is infused. This led to reduction to absurdity when it supposed that the spirit was infused on forty ninth day for males, the eightieth day for females.

The third view, Transducianism, has found equal support in the church. This view holds that parents are responsible not only for the bodies but also the souls of their offspring. Tertullian was an early major advocate. Jerome remarked that the large majority of western thinkers accepted it. Leo the Great maintained it as the doctrine of Catholicism. Augustine maintained a neutral position. (*ISBE*) A related theory (held by G. E. Stall – Berlin – 1734) is that the soul has an activity in forming the body to fit it to its own characteristics. (*ISBE*) Adoptive parents may find considerable evidence for this viewpoint when their adopted children are grown, since psychological studies indicate that adopted children, even those adopted at birth, as adults assume a life style more like their biological parents than their adoptive ones. (Berger) The author's experience with an adopted son and an adopted daughter has followed this pattern, but we are very certain that they both have characteristics that represent our teaching and life style.

Both of the first two theories present problems if you believe in original sin. The view brings up a number of serious questions. Could God create something sinful without being the author of sin? How then, as David (Psalms 51:5) writes, "Behold, I was brought forth in iniquity; and in sin did my mother conceive me." (Many think that the reason Jesse did not bring David to the meeting with Samuel was because David's birth was not legitimate, and it is to this that David refers in the Psalm.) If the impure, sinful body contaminates the soul, why could the soul not decontaminate the body? If every child is a new creation, what happens to continuity with the race? Is Adam purely in physical contact with later generations? This brings up the doctrine of "Original sin." This doctrine first became important with, or was invented by, Augustine of Hippo. If one believes that the guilt for the first sin is inherited, he has difficulty in defending the justice of God. The Scriptures clearly teach that each person is responsible for his own sin (James 1:12—15).

Monism

Accepting philosophical monism forces the thinker to make choices which seem to be nearly ridiculous in our experience and have no Scriptural support. Pure idealism contends that man is only spirit and the body does not actually exist. (Berkley, Mary Baker Eddy) Materialism contends that mind is simply an activity of matter, a product of the brain (Skinner, Pavlov, etc.). This is the view of many modern psychologists. Brightman and Beck (Brightman) answer with the argument that this view is based on a denial of a tremendous amount of data, the whole of human intellectual experience.

The Bible does not deal with these questions as it does not deal with many questions raised by science and philosophy. For example it does not deal with the origin of evil. It does not deal with the origin of spirit or matter except that God created them. (Genesis 1:1—5, John 1:1—5, Colossians 1:15—17) It does not deal with the relation between them. Biblically all of these come from God and are to be accepted as experienced in faith.

The Fall of Man

The Scriptures give us an account of man's fall from paradise into a world of sin, and one in which he in all natural experience becomes a sinner. The Scripture is in marked contrast with the evolutionary approach, which makes man's progress upward. Some evolutionists find leaps, and one is that man failed moral testing, and so sin became dominant in the world.

The effect of the fall included that it brought sin, corruption, and death. We find this both in the Old and New Testaments. It brought death of the body, but not of the spirit. In the end of things both the creation and our bodies will be transformed, renewed. (Romans 8:20—24, Corinthians 15:50—54, 2 Corinthians 5:1—8) The body is not the prison house of the soul as the Platonists held, but a part of creation yet to be redeemed.

The Bible clearly teaches personal responsibility and guilt. (Romans 1: 18—32, especially Verse 20, Romans 2: 1—11, especially Verse 6 and Verse 11 and Romans 12:1, 2) In contrast to this the logical effect of Behaviorism (Pavlov, Skinner, etc.) is that man is conditioned to be what he is, so is not responsible for any of his actions.

The Implications for Psychotherapy

The last statement, that man has guilt and responsibility, may be a basis for rejecting much of the work of Freud. Christianity certainly rejects Behaviorism, since it has no place for a soul or personal responsibility. It also rejects any psychology which supposes a collective consciousness. Though some reject the self-actualization of Maslow, some Christians see the development of the Christian into the image of Christ as the greatest self-actualization.

Mental illness may be a physical organic malfunction: damage, tumors, and gland or chemical disorders. These are diseases and the appropriate treatment is medical.

On the other hand mental illness may be the state of people with personal problems. For these the Bible offers help including a realistic view of sin and guilt, accountability of the person for the actions, (the sin in his life), and provision for confession, forgiveness, reconciliation and sanctification. This has led many Christians into accepting "Reality Therapy" (Glasser) as the best expression of the ministry of God to the mentally disturbed. An example of the application of this theory to Christian counseling is the works of Jay Adams. (Adams) Even Christian counselors often find that the approach of Jay Adams is over simplistic. For persons who are addicted the Bible offers the most comprehensive path to recovery. There is a caution in this that the teachings of the Bible must become part of the mental life of the individual, not simply be verbalized. This may require the efforts of a strong, Biblically competent "helper". The Scriptures ideally provide this "helper" in the shepherd/ teacher (Ephesians 4:11, 12) but few in our day develop the necessary knowledge and skills.

This raises the question of whether a Christian can operate as a counselor when the code of ethics of the profession forbids his communicating his values. Can he be effective or a good steward in God's eyes without teaching values? The Christian believes that the person is a soul and has a body. The Christian believes that the redeemed soul is in eternal life. The Christian has a duty to be considerate of and supporting (in good cases) of the mental states of others. He is concerned to help in improving those mental states into the joy and worry-free life that Paul commands. (Philippians 4: 4—7) Pastoral counseling as opposed to professional counseling offers the freedom to fulfill his divinely required duty as a Christian and at the same time be the "helper" the person needs.

Observations

A Christian Psychologist (or student of Psychology) will operate on the following assumptions and commitments.

1. Persons are souls, destined to unending life or destruction, living in a mortal body.
2. A Christian he will seek to serve these souls in ways that support redemption through Christ.
3. A Christian will extend Christian *agapee* (See the definition of this "love" in earlier chapters.) to every other person.
4. A Christian will believe that every person who is sane is responsible for his actions and should be held accountable for them. He believes that in some cases the person may even be responsible for his "insanity."
5. A Christian will draw from human experience the assistance needed to serve the needs of men's souls, but will carefully judge them (1 John 4:1) against the teaching of divine revelation. (the Scriptures)
6. A Christian will hold that sin and guilt are real and very destructive and can only be removed by repentance coupled with faith and the grace of God in Christ Jesus.
7. A Christian, as a person and in his dealing with persons who have problems, will draw upon his Christian values and resources as an essential part of his work.

CHAPTER 21

SOCIOLOGY, A CHRISTIAN VIEW

Basic Theory

Sociology is the study of the nature and structure of society. We know from Scripture that God created man to be a social being. (Genesis 2:20ff) God ordained institutions. One writer lists these as: labor, marriage, government, the church. The philosophy of "ethical spheres" (Spier) has seven spheres of law which must not meddle in the affairs of the other spheres. The state is the sphere of government. Its purpose is to protect its citizens. The church rules in the area of faith and religious practice. The home controls the area of education. The market place controls commerce, etc.

There are two basically opposed views of society that dominate modern thinking. One maintains that society shapes reality, the other that only individuals can change reality. (Noebel, p. 206) A Christian sociologist sees the individual as more important than any institution devised by man, and considers society an important resource for fulfilling man's need as a social being. (Noebel, p. 206) Individuality and free-will are essential to a Christian view of life, in contrast to the atheistic approach which believes that man's thought and actions are determined by society. (Noebel p. 204) In Christianity man's relationship to God and to the fellowship of the church are his most important social relationships. He must allow himself to be shaped by both of these.

Freedom makes every person and group responsible. The Christian sociologist expects each institution to function in its own area of concern and allow other institutions the same freedom. (Noebel, p. 206) This places the burden of responsibility on man. God rightly blamed Adam and Eve for their sin. Society needs to recognize guilt as a real and build patterns of action to eliminate the items producing guilt. (Noebel, p. 205)

Institutions

The family has always constituted an important and essential part of society. Christians hold that marriage is ordained by God and His ordinances regulate its operation. The USSR attempted to eliminate the family and even this atheist nation found that they could not have an orderly society without it. It is the primary social institution in forming character and personality. The role of parents as care-givers and teachers is an indispensible and an often neglected function of the family.

A second important institution is *the church*. The function of the church in the society includes instructing concerning sin, the necessity of repentance and the means for forgiveness and exhibiting the community which God wants for His people. Paul (1 Corinthians 12:12—31) gives details of the level of involvement God expect in this community. Unfortunately, this duty is too often neglected by today's congregations.

In the Christian view, God instituted *Government*, the third institution to preserve order, but which must rightly be the benevolent servant of the ones governed. In turn the Christian will be submissive to government in so far as that submission does not violate God's commands. The government must not make demands which would cause the citizen to violate God's will. In general the government should deal with protecting its people, and not become involved in other aspects of society.

Additional Observations

The Christian sees society as conditioned by the individuals it contains and recognizes a responsibility as a Christian to influence his society. The Christian believes that the will of God determines right and wrong not the customs of society. Because this is true the Christian will not allow the society to "push him into its mold." Paul forbids this in Romans 12:2. The Christian must by "renewing" his mind transform himself into the likeness of Christ and determine and practice the will of God. We discussed this in the earlier section on Ethics. On the other hand the Christian recognizes that it is his duty to seek to mold the society according to the Biblically prescribed will of God.

Every individual is a part of a network of social groupings. The Christian will find ways of working through this network to fulfill his duty to God.

The Christian has a duty to be a critic of the social order. He as a Christian has a commitment to change that social order into one in harmony with God's will, and to create a social order fulfilling all the needs of the individual. His tool for this will be persuasion, never coercion, since the order is spiritual and coercive physical approaches deal in the wrong area and with the wrong ethic.

The Christian will seek to make the church the social agent and structure prescribed in Scripture. This involves unity of teaching, mutual commitment to God and His will, and a family relation among Christians which provides support of all types for those in need, but especially for fellow Christian.

The Christian will regard the church as the supreme social institution; subject in every way to God's revealed will and the agency developing relationships between people as vitally connected as the parts of the body. (1 Corinthians 12:12—27) He will respect the specialization of the parts as one of its strengths.

A FINAL WORD

This is not a comprehensive statement of a Christian World View, nor is it a scholarly work attempting to set standards in the areas studied. It is simply an effort to help the Christian who is a member of the Body of Christ with a basic orientation to the way that a Christian should look at life.

If you find areas of life that should be added to the study, please contact the author with those suggestions. This is not a completed work, but an effort to fill what seems to be a gap in the literature available to the average church member. It will, I hope, become more comprehensive over the years in later editions. If you study this in a group, I hope that you will encourage discussion and even disagreement where that is appropriate.

Do not consider this the final word in any area. Consider first if the Biblical references are complete and correctly presented. The Word of God is the final authority in all of these matters in so far as it speaks, and what it says is the first and most important consideration.

Do not expect everyone to agree with these statements. Many of them are tentative and open to, in fact welcome further study. At the end of the chapter on "Death" I have quoted from a statement by Alexander Campbell which I believe should be remembered in every discussion which involves generalizations concerning the teaching of Scripture.

Finally, remember that the whole of God's law is based on *agapee* (See my definitions of this "love" earlier in the study.) for Him and our neighbors, particularly fellow Christians.

My graduate students and I have found this a challenging project, but hope that you will continue our efforts in later revisions.

RESOURCES USED

Adams, Jay. *Competent to Counsel.* Grand Rapids, Michigan: Baker Book House, 1970.

_____, *The Christian Counselor's Manual.* Grand Rapids, Michigan: Baker Book House, 1978.

Balmires, Harry. *Recovering the Christian Mind. Meeting the Challenge of Secularism.* 1988.

Baumstarck, Joseph. Dr. Baumstark is a former student and personal friend.

Baxter, Batsell Barrett. *I Believe, Because.* Grand Rapids, Michigan, Baker Book House, 1971.

Berger, Kathleen Stassen. *The Developing Person Through the Life Span.* Worth Publishers, 1994.

Bible, The (ASV). *The Holy Bible, American Standard Version.* New York: Thomas Nelson & Sons, 1901.

Bible, The (ESV). *The English Standard Version.* Wheaton, Ill: Crossway Bibles, 2001.

Bible,The (KJV). *The King James Version.* Indianapolis: Kirkbride, 1934,

Bible, The (NASV). *New American Standard Bible.* Grand Rapids MI: Zondervan, 1985.

Bible, The (NIV). *The New International Version.* Grand Rapids MI: Zondervan, 1973.

Bible, The (The Living Oracles). *The New Testament.* Indianapolis: David Somer, 1912.

Boa, Kenneth. *God, I Don't Understand.* 1975.

Brightman, Edgar Sheffield, and Beck, Robert. *An Introduction to Philosophy.* New York: Henry Holt and Company, 1951.

Brett, Professor. *Brett's History of Psychology.* Edited and abridged by R. S. Peters. Cambridge, Mass.: The Massachusetts Institute of Technology, Press, 1965

Bromley, Geoffrey W. (abridgement of) Kittel, Gerhard, and Fredrich, Gerhard. *Theological Dictionary of the New Testament.* Grand Rapids: Eerdmans Publishing, 1985.

Brown, Francis, D.D., D.Litt. (with the cooperation of doctors S. R. Driver and Charles A.Briggs). *Hebrew and English Lexicon.* Hendrickson Publishers, Inc., 1906, 1996.

Boatman, Russell E. *Beyond Death: What the Bible Says about the Hererafter.* Florisant Missouri: Author, 1980.

_____. *What the Bible Says About the End Times.* Joplin Mo.: College Press Publishing Company, 1980.

Carson-Newman Lectures. Carson-Newman College. About 1970.

Chicago Manual of Style. 15th. edition, Chicago: The University of Chicago Press, 2003.

Compton's Encyclopedia Dictionary. (Incorporating *The Webster's Third International Dictionary Unabridged* and *Seven Languages Dictionary).* Chicago: G. & C. Merriam Co., 1971.

Cottrell, Jack. *Faith's Fundamentals.* Standard Publishing, nd.

_____. *The Faith Once for All.* Joplin, Missouri, College Press Publishing Company, 2003.

_____. *The Authority of the Bible.* Grand Rapids, Michigan: Baker Book House, 1978.

Cubberly, Elwood P. *The History of Education.* Houghton Mifflin Company, 1920, 1948.

Davis, Stephen T. *God, Reason and Theistic Proofs.* 1997.

Ensign, Grayson Harter. *You Can Understand the Bible.* Amarillo Texas: G. and E. Press, 1990,

Fletcher, Joseph E. *Situation Ethics – the New Morality.* Philadelphia: The Westminster Press, 1966.

Foster, Lewis. *Selecting a Translation of the Bible.* Standard Publishing, 1978.

Friedenburg, Edgar Z. *The Vanishing Adolescent.* New York: Dell Publishing Company, 1959.

Geisler, Norman. *Christian Apologetics.* Grand Rapids, Michigan: Baker Book House Company, 1976.

Glasser, William. *Reality Therapy, a New Approach to Psychiatry.* New York: Harper and Row, 1965.

International Standard Bible Encyclopedia. General Editor, James Orr, Grand Rapids: Wm. B. Eerdmans Publishing Co., 1939.

Leman, Kevin. *The Way of the Shepherd: 7 Ancient Secrets to Managing Productive People* Kindle Edition. Grand Rapids, Michigan: Zondervan, 2004.

Johnson, Ashley S. *The Resurrection and the Future Life.* Knoxville: *Knoxville Lithographic, 1913*

Jung, C, G, (Translated by R. F. C. Hull), *Answer to Job.* New York: Meridian Books Inc. 1954.

Lard, Moses E. *Commentary on Paul's Letter to the Romans.* Cincinnati: The Standard Publishing Company, 1875.

Lewis, C. S. *The Four Loves.* This book appears in a number of forms. My best contact with has been with a series of audio tapes narrated by C. S. Lewis himself. In print form it is found in *The Inspirational Writings of C. S. Lewis.* New York: Inspiration Press, 1987.

Lost Books of the Bible. New York: Bell Publishing Company, 1979.

MacArthur, John, editor. *Think Biblically.* Wheaton, Illinois: Crossway Books,2003.

McGarvey, J. W. *Evidences of Christianity.* Cincinnati: Standard Publishing Co., 1886.

Machen, J. Gresham. *New Testament Greek for Beginners.* New York: The Macmillan Company, 1928.

Milligan, Robert. *The Scheme of Redemption.* St. Louis: The Bethany Press, 1960.

Moulton, Harold K. *The Analytical Lexicon.* New York: Harper and Brothers, nd.

Murch, James DeForest, *Christians Only.* Cincinnati: Standard Publishing, 1962.

Noebel, David A. *The Battle for Truth.* Eugene, Oregon: Harvest House Publishers. 2001.

Rawlings, Maruice. *Beyond Death's Door.* Bantam Books, 1979.

Reese, Gareth L. *Romans.* Moberly, Missouri: Scripture Exposition Books, 1996.

Richardson, Robert. *The Memoirs of Alexander Campbell.* Cincinnati: Standard Publishing Company, 1897.

Rice, Mike, Conversations in 2017.

The Septuigent Version of the Old Testament with an English Translation. Grand Rapids: Zondervan 1970.

Shaff-Herzog Encyclopedia of Religious Knowledge. Samuel Macauley Jackson, chef editor. New York: Funk and Wagnalls Company, 1908.

Smith, Wilbur M. *Therefore Stand.* Boston: W. A. Wilde Co., 1945.

Spire. *The Philosophy of Normative Spheres. (Page 32)* (I used this book from the Minnesota Bible College Library in writing papers for the University of Minnesota. I cannot now locate it.)

Stappler, Melissa Conrad, MD. Internet article on miscarriage and still birth.

Sweitzer, Albert. *The Quest of the Historical Jesus.* Great Britain, 1906.

Thayer, Joseph Henry. *Greek English Lexicon of the New Testament.* New York: American Book Company, 1886.

Wallace, Daniel B. *Greek Grammar: Beyond the Basics.* Grand Rapids: Zondervan, 1986.

Webster's New Collegiate Dictionary. Springfield, Mass.: Merriam Co. 1949.

Webster's Third New International Dictionary of the English Language. (Unabridged) Chicago: Encyclopedia Britianica, Inc. 1971.

White, E. B. (Illustrator Garth Williams). *Charlotte's Web.* Harper/ Collins Publishers, 2006.

Printed in the United States
By Bookmasters